HEALING
THROUGH
MANTRA

GW00458633

HEALING
THROUGH
MANTRA

P. KHURRANA

Crest Publishing House

(A JAICO ENTERPRISE)
G-2, 16 Ansari Road, Darya Ganj
New Delhi-110 002

HEALING THROUGH MANTRA
ISBN 81-242-0223-0

First Edition : 2001
Reprinted : 2002

Published by:
CREST PUBLISHING HOUSE
(A Jaico Enterprise)
G-2, 16 Ansari Road, Darya Ganj,
New Delhi-110 002

Printed by:
Saurabh Print-O-Pack
A-16, Sector IV
NOIDA 201301 (UP)

Dedicated
To Her Holiness
My Mother Late Smt. Raj Khurrana

CONTENTS

LIST OF MANTRAS

(x)

(xi)

PREFACE

The present book is an attempt to develop the human potential through Mantra. It deals with what Mantras are, what the benefits of Mantras are, how to use the Mantras and what must be guarded against. Every Mantra has been specified individually alongwith its method, mala, direction, asan and other relevant instructions. Our Indian occult science refers to various Mantras for mitigating various human problems regarding marriage, health, litigation, enmity, politics, children etc. For a particular problem the judicious application of Mantra varies from person to person in accordance to his horoscope; age and sex. Those who want to practice Mantra must seek a true Guru and undertake this spiritual task under his blessings only. The Sadhak should do his duties in the world and worship the deity without selfish motive. He should not acquire wealth and possessions from bad deeds. The aim of writing the book is to bring awareness and understanding of the basic tenets of Mantraism, that flows through mind and soul as spiritual operation for healing, relaxation and stimulation.

—P. Khurrana

ACKNOWLEDGEMENT

At the outset, I would like to express my gratitude to my Gurudev Swami S. Chandra Jee who taught me the religio-magical practices of Mantra-Tantra-Yantra. And also I am credited to all Vedas, Shastras and holy epics of India which have helped me to make use of sound formulae (Mantra) and Diagrams (Yantra), ritual postures (Asans) gestures (Mudras) used as aids to write this book.

I am especially indebted to my saintly father Shri Ram Dass Khurrana who always gave me good sanskaras (Karmas) and disciplined mind.

I thank Ramikka Thakur for her hard work, devotion and efficient managing of my schedule and office.

I especially thank my sister Chandra Kanta for her uninterrupted behaviour and Sat Pal Ji for volunteering his help at most arduous hours of writing the book.

I thank Bill David Tomm who graciously donated remarkable collections of manuscripts on Yoga Sutras and Asans and gave me the opportunity to share freely my ideas with warm support and gesture.

I thank my different promoters and organisers who have put their heart and soul into producing and supporting seminars; lectures; T.V. interviews for me in India and abroad.

The help and support I received from my wife Poonam and my children Ayushman and Aparshakti who have made it possible

ABOUT THE AUTHOR

P. Khurrana better known as modern GURU is a perfect Lord Shiva's devotee, astrologer and occultist who has brought the experience of the truth to the thirsty seekers in other countries also. He is supremely powerful, irresistible and confident.

His contribution and prediction in various magazines and newspapers include "The Sun" "Indian Express", "The Tribune", "The Astrological Magazine", "Rashtriya Sahara" and "The Week".

For him Jyotish and Tantra Mantra is a passion. He puts every effort to illumine the world by his spiritual power. He has been to many countries, delivered countless lectures and given interviews on T.V. and has designed many special programmes on Tantra-Mantra.

P. Khurrana presents his timeless message to everybody that "with meditation, worship and self-realisation Siddhis do come and step by step the Divine Power leads the Sadhakas to higher and higher levels of perfection till he reaches the goal".

To this day who met P. Khurrana always remembers his laughter. The laughter of enlightened being is uncanny. It comes from PARAVANI; the highest level of speech in Mantra which is pure consciousness, the source of perfect sound used in Mantra.

From his pure mind come thousands of devotional episodes about the Truth and God. His devotees are from every walk of life in Inida and abroad. If you ever want to know how to experience the nectar of love, and laughter, you can always turn to him at his residence 36, Sector 12-A, Panchkula (India) where he gives free advice to his devotees on his Gaddi on Sundays only.

for me to lead a normal family life and to have a successful career.

My sincere thanks to my brothers and their devoted wives who adjusted their visits at my ease and understanding.

I thank my critics, friends and associates for their open, honest and supporting sharing of ideas and feedback.

I wish to thank my million of readers and devotees who continue to seek my blessings.

On a personal note, I want to express my thanks to Shri S.C. Sethi, Director, Crest Publishing House, New Delhi who suggested me the title "Healing Through Mantra" and made it possible for you to hold this book in your hands.

Office :   **P. Khurrana**
Hotel Shivalikview
Chandigarh (India)
Phone: 703018, Fax: 701094
Residence: 36, 12-A, Panchkula

WHAT IS MANTRA

Among the several approaches to spiritual power, insight and welfare of man, the cult of Mantras is an important one. There has sprung up in this country an elaborate science of Mantras called Mantra Sastra or Mantra Vidya. The Science has three major divisions Kerala (also called Misdra), Kashmira (called Sattwika) and Gandha (Vama Marga). and it covers not only vedic Hinduism (with its Saiva, Sakta and Vaishnava sub divisions) but Jainism and Buddhism also. The Science has intimate associations with the practice of cosmogramas called Yantra and with the occult rituals known as Tantra.

The Sanskrit expression Mantra is derived from two roots MAN (to think and TRAI (to protect). The general meaning of the word is that of a device by means of which whatever one thinks and attends to with earnestness will protect him from all ills and evils.

A mantra is usually a formula, a collection of letters (or phonemes) of words with or without meaning. Even when the words are meaningful that is as important as the effect its repetition produces. The sounds involved in a Mantra are themselves significant for they generate in the individual an unusual mystic power. The Mantra is expected to reveal its import or deity to the person who works on it. For a Mantra to be effective, therefore, it is prescribed that it must be duly given by a competent master at the most beneficial time, and that it must suit the individual's temperament, eligibility, needs and capacities. A Mantra picked up from books, or casually communicated by another individual will serve no purpose whatever and indeed it may spell harm and ruin. Hence we read.

It becomes a Mantra only when a Guru gives it, otherwise is a group of letters or words and nothing more.

There are, therefore, rules about the constitution of a Mantra, extraction of a Mantra (mantroddhara), visually the import of a Mantra by orderly repetition (puruscharana), sacramental rituals connected with a Mantra (Mantra-Japa), infusing power into the Mantra (mantra Chaitanya), the aspects or several limbs of the Mantra (like armour or kavacha, heart or hirdya, weapon or astra eye or netra), and practice of a mantra (mantra sadhana).

The total number of Mantras available in texts (like Mantra Maharnava, Mantramahodhdhi, Mantra Parijata and Mantra Sarvasava), is said to be seven crores. But most of them are unsuitable for the practice of devotee, for they suffer from disabilities and diseases (which the texts describe as chinna, ruddha, rakta-hina, paranmukha, supta, visirna etc.). A mantra is said to be like an individual and must go through several sequences before it can become effective; janana (birth), dipana (bringing it to light), bodhana (activising), abhisheka (consecration), nirmalikarana (purification), jivana (enlivening), tarpanba (satiations) and aphyayana (completing) the Mantra must be given by the guru who has himself mastered the Mantra by continuous practice. Only one who has realised the importance or the deity of a mantra can give that Mantra to others (hence called 'Mantra Data') and when he gives, the Mantra is already powerful and full of potentialities.

There are, however, some Mantras which are of proven merit, and they are called Siddha-mantra. One who is earnest and disciplined may use the Mantra even when not given by a Guru. Examples are "Om Namo Narayanaya" and "Om Namo Sivaya". The famous Gayatri Mantra also belongs to this category.

These Mantras are generally beneficient to the individual who recite them, but are not calculated to solve and accomplish any desire. They are not in other words, kamyasiddha. For a mantra to be effective in a particular context, it must be specifically and individually communicated by guru.

MANTRA AND MALA

The shastras refer to Mala of 108 beads for enchanting mantra. A longish head is added where two ends of the string are knotted, but while turning the beads one after the another in prayers only the number of 108 beads used. There is a specific guideline that the longish bead at the end should neither be touched nor crossed over. While turning the beads with the tip of the thumb when you reach the end you must not cross over to from where you started but turn back and thus the cycles go on, so that only 108 beads are used. The longish bead at the junction is called "Sumeru" meaning the pinnacle. It is used only to mark the beginning or the end and is not used in the count. What I mean to emphasize is that Hindu shastras regard number of 108 as sacred and sacrosanct.

The number 108 is of great and fundamental significance. 108 is 1+0+8=9. Nine is the last number among the basic numbers. It is the crest of perfection, authority, victory and power because 9 when multiplied by any number always again comes to nine when added i.e. 9, 18, 27, 36, 45, 54, 63 etc. Thus 9 is individual and distinct.

The famous battle of Mahabharata between the Pandavas and the Kauravas lasted for 18 days in the ground of Kurukshetra. (1+8=9) The great epic of Mahabharata covering about one lack shlokas (verses) is divided into 18 paravas (contos). Again (1+8=9) therefore 9 is the highest of the basic numbers; the positive side of which is constructive and the negative is destructive.

To revert to the number of 108 beads in the mala. How is this number arrived at ? what is the logic ? A circle (like a cycle of enchanting Mantra on the mala) has 360 degrees multiplied by 60, it has 21600 minutes in the circle. Hindus shastras reckon the time 60 Ghatis in day and night. (One Ghati is equal to 24 minutes; so the 60 Ghatis come to 24 hours). One Ghati is divided into 60 parts which are called palas. So the 60 Ghatis multiplied by 60 comes to 3600. This further multiplied by 60 (Because a pala = 60 vipalas) comes to 21600. Half of which for the day and half for night comes to 10800. Obviously this number would be too large for practical use and so we drop the zeros and employ a mala with 108 beads.

It is to coordinate the rhythm of time and space that we use the number of 108 so that it may be in harmony with the spiritual powers of nature which is known as almighty the God, the supreme.

I have referred to the 108 beads of the mala used by the Hindus. But in certain specified purposes the mala of different number of beads is used. Tantrik writings refer that if one wants to pray for the salvation of the soul he should use the mala with 25 beads. For those who want to attain health and riches, mala which has 30 beads has to be used. The mala with 27 beads may be used for generally all objects, but if you want to annihilate your enemy, you should use a mala with 15 beads. A mala which has 54 beads may be used for the fulfilment of various desires. The mala having 108 beads is a perfect one and suitable for all purposes. The use of mala is mentioned below.

Mala of Pearl and Lotus Beads: Mala of pearl and lotus beads is used for the removal of evil effects caused by the evil deities, alleviating diseases and for begetting son. Chanting with the help of a mala of pearl will produce the result one lakh time more.

Mala of Rudraksh Beads: This mala is used for Ucchhattan of causing injury and destruction of enemies.

Mala of Five Flowers: Mala made of five different coloured flowers—white, red, yellow, black and green flowers are considered the best for the attainment of all auspicious siddhis.

Counting by Fingers: Use of fingers for counting gives ten times more results.

Mala of Aamvala: Recitation with the help of mala of Aamvala gives one thousand more beneficial results.

Mala of Long : Results are five thousand times more if one does the chanting of mantra with the help of a mala of Long.

Mala of Gold Balls: Results are one crore times more if one does the chanting of mantra with the help of a mala of gold balls.

In the absence of mala one can enchant the "Mantra" by the use of fingers.

ANKUTA (Thumb) is used for final emancipation, TARAJANI (Jupiter finger) for the prosperity through trading or business, MADHYAMA (2nd or finger of Saturn) for wealth and happiness, Anamika (finger of Sun) for peace and finally KANISHTA (4th or finger of Mercury) is for all the types of Mantra Siddhi. For inflicting injury or destroying or finishing off an enemy Tarajani (finger of Jupiter) is the best.

MANTRA, SADHANA AND KARMA

I have come across lot of people from every walk of life from India and abroad who have read a lot about Yantra-Mantra and Tantra but complain that they have not achieved anything. Rather I have found them saying Mantras are nothing but misguiding the people. Basically people with wrong motives pretend to be Sadhakas and adopt short cut methods to attain worldly goals without taking much pain during meditation, whereas meditation is purely an art of concentration and one needs a strong intutional power.

Basically the Sadhaka (The practitioner) for the successful accomplishment of Mantra Siddhi must develop his intutional power with regular practice of self-introspection and keep his mind clear from various doubts and impressions.

Creating pressure on the mind, he has to develop a calm, and cool mind with lot of peaceful energy-charge. This may give the Sadhaka a self-intoxication. Detach your mind from the materialistic pursuits where everyone is running fast to earn more and more money. That is why in olden time the Sadhana was limited to only Rishis who used to spend many years far from the world near the mountains and rivers.

A modern Sadhaka must relax, conquer tiredness of mind, feel happy, cheerful and enjoy a good healthy life. Aloneness, self-seclusion and your own confidence will increase your intutional power to a great extent. Impatience is Sadhaka's greatest enemy and it will make infirm spiritual health. You are a great powerful soul. Your expression will prove true. Your patience and sincere efforts will bring results. You can change destiny of anyone by simple wish. Sometimes being innocent and pure. Your personality gets hooked by very clever worldly people who catch you, touch your feet and put pressure on your mind for their selfish unlawful motives. So attach no importance to anyone. Just bless them and leave the things to God because truth alone wins.

Now the question is "Can a Sadhaka heal everybody through Mantra?" Basically Mantra, Sadhana and Karma are inter-linked. When Sadhana is done with total morality with no desire for the fruits is known as good Karma which ultimately leads to high stage of Yogic development and the Sadhaka enjoys the support of the people. His power becomes so Divine that he gets the capacity to heal not every human but the animals too. When the Sadhana is done with indiscipline and selfish motive it is treated as "Bad Karma" which ultimately leads towards endless sufferings and divine punishment. These people then turn to be unholy and quacks.

It is the main Karma of a successful and conscientious Sadhak not to turn his clients into fatalists Sadhaks or self-styled Tantrik with low breeding can be seen in metropolitan cities some of them even claiming to be very near to Ministers and VIPs. They have had a very low level of education. Without having a proper educational background these Tantriks can only be charlatans. Yet these Tantriks dominate the scene because they steal the lime light due to close association with corrupt politicians and because of their saffron hypocritical Dhoti-Kurta.

A morally upright Sadhak sees in Vedas the truth which is discovered in Mantras and Yogic meditation. This Karma leads the Sadhak on to higher spiritual aspiration. The original purpose of the Sadhak is to serve the mankind. A Sadhaka must believe that it is only God's law of truth and logic which must prevail. Only Karma prevails.

A good Karma and proper principle for Sadhana must be followed which are given below:

(1) A good Jupiter, or the Uranus the planets of Mantra and Mystery respectively is necessary for a Sadhak.

(2) A Sadhak without the blessing of GURU can accomplish nothing.

(3) Purify your body with proper bath and enchant following purificatory Mantra on Thursday before starting Sadhana.

AUM HRIN ARHAM SRI JIN-PRA-BHANJAN MUM KARM-BHASM VIDHUNAN-NAN KURU KURU SAWAHAA

While taking the bath and recitation of Mantra you must think that: My entire Sins and Akarmas have been destroyed.

(4) Avoid, sex, anger, lust cruel people and emotion.

(5) Correct use of Asna, Mudra, Mala and code should be followed under the guidance of your Guru.

(6) While reciting the Mantra the diction should be clear and perfect.

(7) The purpose of Sadhna must be clear and positive.

(8) The Mantras of Maaran, Uchhattann and Vashikaran can bring ill effects. Sadhakas are advised to use them in rare cases or in self-defence under strict supervision of Guru.

(9) During the Sadhana; if you see any supernatural miracle; be at ease and have strong determination to face it.

(10) The Sadhak should keep on purified vegetarian food. Intoxication must be avoided.

(11) Asthra Assan is the best posture for any Mantra Shakti whereas Kaaryothsrag is the best posture if Sadhak is to perform while standing in the water. These are the most comfortable assans which keep Sadhak's mind and body in complete order.

(12) Sadhak must maintain the secrecy.

I appeal all seekers of truth (Sadhaks) to discipline their habits and body for good results. Your mind must be trained to tolerate the sufferings of people by regular Shan Asna, exercise and keeping mum (MAUN VRAT) for hours together otherwise you cannot have the power to ameliorate the sufferings of the people.

My clients normally question "How do you read human minds and solve their problems so quickly. What is the mystery of your Divine Power"?

I simply rely, "This is all by the grace of Lord Shiva and my Guru Swami S. Chandra Ji who have bestowed me intutional, telepathic and healing powers".

THE POWER OF SOUND

The Vedas stated that seers and Maharishis had the power to see the meaning of the uttered Mantras. "Mantra" is a purposeful sound one makes to establish contact or link between the inner force and the outer force. All the external sounds which we perceive are created when two or more objects such as vocal cords, strike together and set up a vibration in the atmosphere. These vibrations then enter the ear through setting up vibrations in the ear-drum and its fluid. The native of these vibrations is relayed to the brain where they are acknowledged and compared to the memory of all past sounds and mental thigmotropic is then created. In this way sound is continuously effecting our minds.

Once Swami Ramakrishna was addressing a large gathering and telling them about the power of sound and mantra. He said that even utterance produces a specific effect on the mind and its functioning. He said by repeating RAMA, RAMA, RAMA . . . . one can realise the existence of God and you can purify your mind. All of a sudden a self opinionated surgeon of high status stood proudly and said sarcastically to Ramakrishan "You ask us to repeat the name of Rama and say that we will realise the God that way. What rubbish, how it is possible? he added slightingly "if you are hungry, would your stomach be filled by repeating Roti, Roti, Roti . . . . ? If it could, I would agree that God can be realized by repeating Rama, Rama, Rama ..."

The noble Ramakrishna who never abused any one, said to the surgeon with anger, "You rascal, son of bitch, do not argue, and sit down".

The moment that learned surgeon heared such words unexpectedly his composure vanished. His face turned red, his blood began to boil, his eyes shot fire. The surgeon was highly acclaimed because of his abilities, degrees and attainment. He was furious on Swami's remarks. The surgeon became more enraged when Ramakrishna taking pity, looked towards him and said "please try to be calm, you are ignorant".

"You are asking me to be calm. You have insulted me before everyone in foul terms and asking me to stay calm?". The surgeon was egoistic.

Then Ramakrishna said "please let me know what has happened, after all where is my fault?".

"You dare to pretend, and you don't know what has happened. I am a surgeon of high status and you have publicly called me a son of bitch, yet you ask me to hold my peace."

Ramakrishna then began to explain, "Look, I never meant to abuse you. I only answered your question in the manner it was put. You said one cannot fill one's stomach just by repeating Roti, Roti, Roti . . . Well I used one word and it has changed you entirely. You have turned red and probably out of rage. This is the effect of one single word. When an ordinary word of abuse can have such an effect, what makes you think that the Divine name Rama will not have? The surgeon realised the power of divinity and was at once silenced.

This example of Swami Ramakrishna brings forth the fact that countless people are unaware about the power, strength and spirit of sound which communicates manifold meaning for specific Mantra. Therefore, the sound is very realistic, and logical. From vision and experience our ancient rishies have fixed up certain sounds to achieve particular purposes. These are called "Beeja Mantra". For instance the sound of AUM is meant for spiritual upliftment, the sound of "ARHAM" for mental peace, the sound of "GLONG" for harmony or the sound of "AUM SHRIN" for prosperity and so on. The rationale of reciting Mantra is that the SOUND created by them vibrates in the cosmos and draws back the cosmic force desired. The other rationale is that vibrations of Sound create desired reactions with the body and mind itself.

VIBRATION OF VARIOUS DHWANIS (SOUND)

Sounds: There are three kinds of sounds:

1. Savitra

2. Anudatta

3. Udatta

Savitra is the mixed tone produced by the combination of high and low tone. When Savitra is raised i.e. when it is uttered with more sound Udatta is produced, whereas Anuddata is low and grave sound. In each of the three accents mentioned above there are seven separate notes widely known as "SAPTA SWARAS" which are called:

1. Shadja—known as peacock

2. Rishabha—known as notes of bull

3. Gandhara—known as notes of goat

4. Madhyama—known as notes of curlew or hiren

5. Pancama—Known as notes of koil

6. Dhaivata—Known as notes of horse

7. Nishada—Known as notes of elephants

Sound is actually produced by the first letters or syllables; thus the flow of the sound is like SHA being pronounced first and NI at the end; SHA-RI-GA-MA-PA-DHA-NI.

I have narrated in the preceding pages the power of sound; the words are 48 which are used in the different Mantras. What they mean while vibrate is detailed below.

(A) : A man standing upright; denotes initiative and leadership; a naughty person; black, authoritative and male. Creator of pranava Beeja.

(AA) : A strong will; determined and aggressive, creator of Maaya Beeja; bearer of serpant and elephants.

(E) : Lord Indra of Hindu mythology; bestower of power and prosperity; builder and architect of greater things.

(EE) : Female with supernatural power; Essence of Amrita Beeja; powerful in carrying out knowledge; possessor of magical weapons.

(U) : Visualiser of enmity and cruelty; producer of Uccahhattan Beeja; splendid in destruction.

(UU) : Unconventional; 'enunch'; indicator of Ucchataka Beeja; capable of destroying enemy; splendid optimistic outlook.

(RI) : Visualises graveyard; produces energy and excitement for occultism (Siddhi); popular in the minds of Sadhakas; symbolises advance studies.

(LRU) : Hindu Kshtriyi performer of Yajna; origin of Lakshmi Beeja; denotes self study and gift of meditation.

(AE) : Maha Vishnu of Hindu mythology; person wearing Saffron clothes and mala of lotus; shows keen intutional and mystical depth; stands for protection.

(AEY) : Vehicle of Lord Vishnu; seated in triangular Asan; supreme; creator of Vashikaran Beeja; keen to take bath in pure milk; A pillar of light in the darkness.

(O) : Origin of Maya Beeja; seated in Padmasan; worshipper of Lord Vishnu and Lord Shiva; Goddess Lakshmi; messenger of peace and prosperity; shows universal tolerance.

(OW) : Supreme in Ucchatan and Maaran Beeja; Signifies success to destroy evil spirits.

(AAN) : Religious Hindu wearer of Jneu; (a sacred thread); magnetic in Mantra recitation; root of all Mantras. Origin of Lakshmi Beeja and Aakaash Beeja.

(AA) : Seated in triangular Asan in repelling position; root of Shanti Beeja indicates stamina; strength and endurance with sative taste.

(KA) : Jata Dhari magnificient look; origin of Shanti Beeja and Kaam Beeja; Male sex; shows a sunny disposition combined with joy and fame.

(KHA) : Kashtriya male sex; Origin of Akash Beeja; Ucchhattan Beeja; highly developed intution in Tantra and Siddhi.

(GA) : Great enlightenment in ornaments and Divine power. Origin of Maya Beeja.

(GHA) : Kashatriya with Tantric Siddhi; Origin in Mohak Beeja and Maaran Beeja; Protector of enemies.

(NGA) : Unconventional, Armed and Ugly; destroyer origin of Vidmaska Beeja and Maathrka Beeja.

(CHA) : Endowed with highest ideals and mercurial qualities. Origin of Ucchattan Beeja; a spark of brilliance and ability.

(CHHA) :Mythologically a vehicle of Lord Vishnu; stands for eternal and spiritual duties; capable of furious acts.

(JA) : Lord Varuna; shudra, male sex; truthful, origin of Shree Beeja.

(Jha) : Kubera; truthful wearer of Shankh (Conch) and mala of pearls; stands for vision and foresight.

(JHA) : Male unmoral, possessor of Trishul and Axe; symbolizes the law of self preservation; denotes caution.

(TA) : Slow and steady connected with the Moon; origin of Bahri Beeja; provides protection in religious rites.

(THA) : Kashtriya male sex; origin of Bahri Beeja; great power of discrimination and destruction; not a good omen.

(DA) : Indicates character of beauty and magnetic qualities; protector of material and spiritual things; stands firmly with weapons.

(DHA) : Magnificent; charming; male; roars like a lion; creator of Maaran Beeja and Maya Beeja; Capable of reacting highest human aspiration.

(NNA) : Origin of Sarva Siddhi, sitting on triangular Asan with Trishul as weapon; spark of Divine imagination.

(TTA) : Male with good fragrance; dominating astral vibrations; symbolizes Sarv Siddhi in combination with Sarawastha Beeja; imbued with great magnetism.

(THA) : Lord of fire; Jata Mukhi Dhari; gives strength to Lakshmi Beeja.

(DA) : Dominating the Lord of death (YAMA) black colour; symbol of wrong determination; destroyer of Karma.

(DHA) : Jata Mukut Dhari; foul smell; black colour; originating Maaya Beeja; accepts human values.

(Na) : Dominating the Lord of Death (Yama) armed with trishul; symbol of strong determination; originator of five elements (Tatavas).

(PA) : Lotus posture; male sex; ornamental; dominating all the deities; stands for prosperity and power with great personal magnetism.

(PHA) : Its sound signifies PAT for Ucchattan; symbolizes male sex; destroyer of enemies; indicates occult powers for constructive and destructive things.

(BA) : Dominating the Lord of Wealth (KUBERA); Wearer of shank (Conch) possessor of controllable and uncontrollable forces.

(BHA) : Unconventional, shrewed and shunned by the society; worshipped by Rahu; Enunch; Its sound signifies Maaran and Ucchattan.

(MA) : Worshipped by Lord of fire (AGNI); symbol of the rising Sun and Padmasana; an orderly mind for Mantra; systematic for success and harmony in home.

(YA) : Creator of all beings; romantic and quixotic symbolizes great enlightenment in recitation of Mantra and fulfilment of desires; shows highly developed intution to Sadhak.

(RA) : Triangular posture; worshipped by Lord of Fire (Agni); Power of Mantra in all the planets; has extremely powerful sound in world of Mantra Siddhi.

(LA) : Worshipped by Lord Indra with Trishul as weapon; its sound (KLAN-KUN) in Mantra is significant for attainment of wealth.

(VA) : Worshipped by Lord Varuna; its sound is significant for Siddhi/supernatural powers (JADOO-TONA).

(SHA) : Jat-Mukuta-Dhari with Lotus weapons symbolises personal magnetism. Its sound is significant for constructive things.

(SSHA) : Male sex with sour taste; its sound is significant for putting out fire; indicates occult power (Siddhi) for destructive things.

(SA) : Worshipped by Lord of wealth (KUBERA); male sex; it is a powerful sound in the world of Siddhi, Mantra, Tantra and Music.

(HA) : Worshipped by all Gods; most prominent sound like SA, RE, GA, MA; it has extremely powerful vibrations when used in the beginning of Mantra followed by RA i.e. HRAN, HRIN, HRON.

(KSHA) : Worshipped by Lord of Fire (AGNI) and Lord Shiva; Male sex; Jata-Mukuta-Dhari; it has extremely Powerful vibrations when used in the Mantra.

VOWELS IN NAGRI-LIPI AND ITS EQUIVALENT IN ENGLISH LANGUAGE

A	a as in Sita oral
Aa	a as in bar barber
Yei	I as in bill lilly
Yee	I as in Polish
Oa	u as in pull push
Oo	u as in rude attitude
Ri	ri as in merily
Ree	ri as in marine
Lri	Lri as in revelry
Lree	Lri as in revelry i.e. prolonged
Ye	e as in prey here
Yei	a as in aisle
o	as in slow stone
Own	au as in Haus
Ama	Nasal sound 'M'
A:	h symbol called visarga
K	k-k in keen
Kh	Kh-ckh in blockhead

G	g-g(hard) in go
Gh	gh-gh in long-hut
N	n-ng in singer
Ch	c-ch (not k) chain
Chh	ch-chh in catch him
J	j-j in judge
Jh	jh-dgeh in hedgeehog
n	n-n (somewhat) as in french
T	t-t in tn
Th	th-th in anti hill
D	d-d- in deen
Dh	dh-dh in godhood
Ne	n-n in under
T	t-t- in three
Th	th-th in thumb
D	d-th in then
Dh	dh-then in breathe
N	n-n in not
P	p-p in pen
Ph	ph-ph in loophole
B	b-b in bag
Bh	bh-bh in abohar
M	m-m in mother
Y	y-y in yard
R	r-r in run

L	l-l in luck
V	v-v- in avert
Sh	s-sh in reich (German)
SHA	s-sh in show
S	s in Sun
H	h in hot
	m-m in sum
	h-h in half

MANTRA AND PLANETS

In this mathematical universe everything is controlled by the great planets which is termed as TIME (KAAL); the supreme Destroyer. In the womb of time everything comes into existence or as it is said that destiny cannot be changed.

The ancient Maharishis meditated deep into the matter and gave us the great science of Occultism (Mantra-Tantra-Yantra). An astrologer sometimes is helpless to world of the malefic influence of planets. Then comes "Mantra" the practical application of occult forces, to avert evil propensities of the planetary influences. "Mantras" prescribe various rites and remedies to curb the evil planetary forces for the well-being of man. Now I will combine the truth of astrology with the power of Mantra to get a full view of the mundane existence and, thereby we can help overselves to swim over the riddles of life peacefully.

Time (Kaal) is divided into nine parts in accordance with the nine planets. The Sun, Moon, Mars, Rahu, Jupiter, Saturn, Mercury, Ketu, Venus and the nine planetary agencies through which time enforces its possibilities on the life of man. In the horoscope we see that planets act as the torch-bearers through which we can see our future promptly. At certain situations man cannot mould his future by the strong malefic effects of the planets. Man is just helpless waiting for the auspicious time or expecting a good Dasa-factor of planets.

But Mantra tells us that any evil tendency of planets can be curbed by recitation of Mantra which balance the harmony of the temporal order in an occult way. Any disharmony, caused by our past actions or malefic planets can be nullified by the power of Mantra.

Starting from the Sun the planet for life we can see that Sun-Dasa for 6 years will commence if the native runs the period of three stars i.e. KRITTIKA, UTTARAPHALGUNI and UTTARASADHA respectively. Evil configuration of planets in these stars will affect the native adversely during Sun-Dasa if not properly pacified. Similarly Moon-Dasa on 10 years will be experienced due to the effect of three stars i.e. ROHINI, HASTA and SHRAVANA collectively. Adverse situation of planets in those stars will affect the native during Moon-Dasa if not properly harnessed. In this manner the 27 stars of Zodiac will throw their influences during nine planetary periods starting from the Sun and ending with Venus is BHIMSOTTARI-DASA system.

Now I will explain the relations of planets with Mantra in specific manner.

(1) SUN—the creator is radiant-expanding and possess life giving qualities. It is represented by the letter "AUM" which has the quality of creation in parallel to the Sun God. Hence, any adverse effect of Sun Dasa can be diverted by "AUM" Japa Pranab Purashcharan effectively. Surya Narayan Home with Surya-Kavach to eradicate the adversity of Sun-Dasa in a Mantric manner.

(2) MOON—a passive, luminous and mind controlling planet which is represented by the Mantric Syllable "HRIN". This is called Maya-Beeja or Sakti-Beeja. The presiding deity is Goddess Bhubaneshwari. Hence Bhubaneshwari Kavach Japa and Homa is fit for pacification of Moon which has connection with the mental plane.

(3) MARS—the commander of the God is fierce, hot and energetic. It gives protection to the Divine Kingdom. It is also the body which fights against diseases and enemies. The Mantric syllable "Hleen" on Bagalamukhi Beeja is Tantric parlance which protects man from danger. Hence "Hleen" Japa Bagla Kavach and Homa is proper for adversities of the planet Mars.

(4) MERCURY—the planet of intelligence rules over brain and nerves centers. The Mantric Syllable "AIM" or there Sarswati Beeja is recited for Mercurial affliction. The Saraswati-Beeja enriches the brain and intellectual faculties. The Sarswati Kawach and Homa are prescribed for Mercurial disturbances.

(5) JUPITER—the Guru is massive planet which is like a second Sun. It has the properties of radiance and it can save man at the last of his hope. The Mantric Syllable "Strin" or Shanti-Beeja is prescribed for JOVECAL affliction which has the qualities of growth and expansion. He is also called the Tara-Beeja which gives light in the darkness. The Tara Kavach and Homa are performed for jupiterical disorders.

(6) VENUS—the beautiful and pleasant planet influences the worldly comforts and luxury. The Mantra Syllable "Shrin" on Laxmi-Beeja is recited for Venusian enrichment, Goddess of wealth and beauty. (Also known as Goddess of 3W, wealth, women and wine). KAMALA is the presiding deity and Kamala Kavach and Homa is used for any Venusian disturbance.

(7) SATURN—the destroyer is regarded as the embodiment of suffering and pain in life. It detaches man from worldly connections and attaches the soul with the higher self. Any such afflictions of Saturn can be pacified with "Krin" Japa, Kali Kavach and Kalika. Homa is properly performed.

(8) RAHU—the planet Rahu is the embodiment of sensual fulfillment. All the five senses grow harmoniously if Rahu is well placed in the Horoscope. Any adverse aspect to Rahu will make the native a slave to senses. The Mantric Syllable "Klin" or Kawa Beeja is fitted for pacification of Rahu as this Beeja will expand the Senses harmoniously to enjoy the material objects. "Klin" Japa, Krishna.

(9) KETU—the last planet Ketu is serpent which has no head. Hence Ketu is the body without head. It is hot, blind and radiates poison all over the world. The mantric Syllable "Trin" or Teja Beeja is prescribed for the planet Ketu. This is the seed of fire which burn everything into a non-existent state. Ketu is pacified by "Trin" Japa and Dhumabat Kavach and Homa.

You will find more Mantras for specific planets in the following pages. From the above one thing is sure that planets and mantras have close proximity. My deep investigation and research underline that "Planets only impel whereas Mantras compel".

GAYATRI MANTRA

It is believed that during cosmic dissolution the Universe merged in AUM. AUM has no beginning or end. It is beyond time, space and causation.

AUM is expressed through Praana-vayu or the vital breath by men. Hence it is called PRANAVE BEEJA. In every breath man utters it. repeats it unintentionally and inevitably AUM is the quest and search of all saints.

If one goes to the page of any Mantra, AUM is the basic sound. Without recitation of AUM no mantra is complete. All the vedic Mantras have emerged from AUM. Likewise Om is the basic necessity of Gayatri Mantra. Because AUM is Gayatri.

Brahma the creator thought of giving one single Mantra which is common to all. Hence Brahma created Gayatri Mantra as mentioned below:

AUM Bhoor Bhuva Svah: Tat Savitur Vareenyam
Bhargo Devasya Dheemahi;
Dhiyo Yo Nah Prachodayaat

The essence of this Mantra is that through this Mantra one requests the supreme to enlighten the intellect. Actually this Mantra praises the glory of HIM and reminds HIM that HE is the remover of all sins and ignorance. So to come to the rescue of the human beings, Brahma created the Mantra.

Let us analyze word by word meaning of the above MANTRA:

AUM	The ultimate; HIM; God
Bhoor	The eternal
Bhuvah	The creator
Svah	Independent
Tat	The eternal
Savitur	The creative principle of light manifesting through the Sun
Varnyam	The supreme God propitiated by the highest Gods
Bhargo	The light that bestows wisdom, bliss, the everlasting life.
Devasya	The light of God
Dheemahi	We meditate
Dhiyo	Intellect
Yo	Who our
Nah	May lead
Prachodayaat	Towards illumination

Who brought Gayatri to the earth: as per the universally accepted belief Sage Viswamitra brought Gayatri to the earth.

AUM Bhu, AUM Bhuvah, AUM Svaa, AUM Mahaa AUM Janah, AUM Tapah, AUM Satyam, AUM Tat Savitur Varenyam Bhargo Devasya Dheemahi Dhiyo YO Nah Prachodayat.

AUM Apo Jyothi Raso-mritam Brahmaa Bhur Bhuvah Swaa AUM

It is also believed that Gayatri was worshipped by the Trinities (Brahma, Vishnu and Shiva) as the mother.

Gayátri is to be recited early morning and evening. It is also called Sandhya Vandana. Sandhya means the junction period of day and night i.e. dawn and dusk as also dusk and dawn, which means early morning and early evening. These periods of exhalation are balanced during these hours and Dhyana (meditation) or concentration becomes profound and peaceful.

According to Manu, the law maker, Gayatri meditation and recitation done just before sunrise is supreme. Similarly meditation or recitation done exactly during sunset is also considered supreme. No food is to be taken before the Gayatri meditation in the morning.

If one wants to do Gayatri Sadhana i.e. attaining complete hold over the Gayatri, one has to undergo several steps; which are mentioned below:

1. Use mala of Rudraaksha or Sandalwood beads.

2. Sit for meditation facing the East in the morning.

3. Before you bathe, apply oil mixed with Haldi (turmeric) powder all over your body and then take bath.

4. Take bath with milk before meditation.

5. Spread a yellow cloth on the seat where you sit for meditation.

6. Keep the photo of Gayatri or Savitri before you.

7. The meditation should be at a permanent place which should be kept neat, calm and sacred.

8. Give oblation of Ghee into the fire simultaneously chanting Swaaha after reciting the Gaayatri Mantra.

9. Minimum number of continuous recitation of Gayatri Mantra is 21 times and minimum days are 21 days.

THE TWELVE SUN MANTRAS

Every year the Sun passes through twelve different phases, known as, the zodiacal signs in western astrology, and as the Rashis in Hindu astrology. According to Hindu astrology, each Rashi has specific attributes or moods, and in each of these twelve moods, the Sun is given a different name. These twelve names comprise the twelve Sun Mantras, which are to be mentally repeated in their respective order in conjunction with the twelve movements of Surya Namaskara. These sun Mantras are not merely names of the Sun, but every sound syllable contained in them is the vehicle of a basic, eternal energy (Shakti) represented by the Sun itself. By repetition and concentration on these mantras, the whole mental structure will benefit and be uplifted.

Although these mantras do not require intellectual understanding, a translation of their meaning is given below for those with an inquiring mind as well as for the more spiritually inclined who wish to use the mantras as a form of attainment with the source of spiritual illumination symbolized by the Sun.

1. AUM MITRAYA NAMEH:
(salutations to the friend of all)

The first position, parnamasana, embodies the attitude of reverence to the source of all life as we know it: the Sun is regarded as the universal friend, endlessly giving light, heat and energy to support this and all other planets. In the scriptures, Mitra is desribed as calling men to activity, sustaining earth and sky, and beholding all creatures without discrimination, just as the early morning Sun signals the beginning of the day's activities and sheds its light on all life.

2. AUM RAVAYE NAMEH:
(salutations to the shining one)

Ravaye means one who shines and offers divine blessing upon all life. In the second position, hasta uttanasana, we are stretching our whole being upwards, towards the source of light, to receive these blessings.

3. AUM SURAYAYE NAMEH
(salutations to He who induces activity)

Here the Sun is in a very dynamic aspect as the deity, Surya. In ancient vedic mythology, Surya was worshipped as the lord of the heavens, pictured crossing the sky in his fiery chariot, drawn by seven horses. This is a beautiful analogy and needs a correct interpretation. The seven horses actually represent the seven rays or emanations of the supreme consciousness, which manifest as the seven planes of existence. Bhu (earthly, material), bhuvar (intermediate, astral) suwar (subtle, heavenly), mahar (the abode of the devas), janah (the abode of divine souls who have transcended ego), tapah (the abode of enlightened siddhas) and satyam (the ultimate truth of reality). Surya symbolizes the supreme consciousness itself, in control of all these different planes of manifestation. Surya is regarded as the most concrete of the solar Gods, of the original vedic triad, his place being in the sky, while Agni (fire) is his representative on earth.

4. AUM BHANAVE NAMEH:
(Salutations to HE who illumines)

The Sun is the physical representation of the guru or teacher, who removes the darkness of our delusions, just as the darkness of the night is removed with every dawn. In the fourth position,

ashwa sanchalanasana, we turn our face towards this illumination
and pray for end to the dark night of ignorance.

5. AUM KHAGAYA NAMEH:
(Salutations to the one who moves through the sky)

It is the Sun's daily movement through the sky which is
the basis of our measurement of time, from the earliest use of
a Sun-dial to the sophisticated devices used today. In Parvatasana,
we offer obeisances to the one by whom time is measured, and
pray for progress in life.

6. AUM PUSHNE NAMAHE:
(Salutations to the giver of strength and nourishment)

The Sun is the source of all strength. Like a father, he
nourishes us with energy, light and life. We offer respect in
asthanga namaskara by touching all the eight corners of our
body to the ground; in essence we are offering our whole
being in the hope that he may bestow mental, physical and
spiritual strength and nourishment upon us.

7. AUM HIRANYA GARBHAEE NAMEH:
(Salutations to the Godemic cosmic self)

Hiranya Garbha is also known as the golden egg, resplend-
ent as the Sun, in which Brahma was born as the manifestation
of self existence. Hiranya Garbha is the seed of causality, thus
the whole universe is contained within Hirnaya Garbha in the
potential state prior to manifestation. In the same way, all life
is potential in the Sun, which represent the great cosmic principle.
We offer respect to the Sun in bhujangasana, the seventh position,
praying for the awakening of creativity.

8. AUM MARICHAYE NAMEH:
(Salutations to the Rays of the Sun)

Maricha is one of Brahma's sons just as the rays of light
are produced from the Sun, but his name also means Mirage,

for our whole life, we seek after a true meaning or purpose, like the thirsty man seeks water in a desert, but is fooled by mirages dancing on the horizon produced by the Sun's rays. In the eighth position, Parvatasana, we pray for true illumination and discrimination in order to be able to distinguish between the real and unreal.

9. AUM ADITYAYA NAMEH:
(Salutations to the Son of Aditi)

Aditi is one of the many names given to the cosmic mother, Mahashakti. She is the mother of all the Gods, boundless and inexhaustible, the creative power from which all divisions of power poroceed. The Sun is one of her children, or manifestations. In the ninth position, ashwa sanchalanasana, we salute Aditi, the infinite cosmic mother.

10. AUM SAVITE NAMEH:
(Salutations to the stimulating power of the Sun)

Savitre is known as the stimulator, one who arouses, and is often associated with Surya who also represents the Sun before rising, stimulating and arousing man into walking activity, and Surya is said to represent the Sun after Sunrise, when activity begins. Therefore in the tenth position, Padahastasana, we salute Savitre in order to obtain the vivifying power of the Sun.

11. AUM ARKAYE NAMEH:
(Salutation to HE who is fit to be praised)

Arka means energy. The Sun is the source of most of the energy in the world, we know. In the eleventh position, hasta uttanasana, we are offering respects to this source of life and energy.

12. AUM BHASKARAYA NAMEH:
(Salutations to the one who leads to enlightenment)

In this final salutation, we offer respects to the Sun as a symbol of the great reveler of all transcedental and spiritual truths. He lights up the pathway leading to our ultimate goal of liberation. In the twelfth position, pranamasana, we pray that this pathway may be revealed to us.

MANTRA AND GEMS

Indeed Gem Therapy or study of stones is one of the oldest science known to mankind. As many of my readers may know little or nothing about the use of gems, because in astrology gem therapy itself is a complete subject and its study is deep and mysterious, I am giving a brief introduction about it here.

I have come across lot of people who complain that gems worn by them have not brought any visible effect in their career. Basically gems should be prescribed on the basis of complete calculation of horoscope wherein name, date of birth, time and place of birth is required. These gems are suggested for a particular problem like marriage, love, litigation, health, studies, fear, poverty, speculation, foreign travel, political elevation and general prosperity etc. These gems/stones are known as lucky stones which bring god luck and fortune for a particular cause mentioned above.

There are thousand of variety of gems in the world. However, the learned have given importance to only 84 types of gems. These 84 types of gems have further been reduced to nine in order of merit. The nine important gems which are called as NAVARATNAs are Ruby, Pearl, Emerald, Coral, Blue Sapphire, Pukhraaj, Gomed and Lahsuniya.

RUBY (MANIK)

Ruby is of planet Sun. Person with Simha (Leo) Rashi should wear this gem. Person in whose horoscope the Sun is not placed well, he can also wear this.

Method of wearing: Ruby should be between 4¼ Ratti to 10¼ Ratti in weight. The day to be selected for wearing is 1st, 6th, 10th or 28th day of your birth month or on Sunday morning. This can be worn on neck, arms or on Sun finger of right hand irrespective of the fact that the wearer is a male or a female. Ruby may be fixed in gold.

Mantra for wearing Ruby

Recite the following mantra 11 times by holding Ruby in your hand and wear.

AUM Aakrshnena Rajasaa Varthamaanom
Niveshyannamrtham Marthyanja.
Hiranyena Savithaa Rathenaa-devo Yaathi
Bhuvanaani Pashyathu.

MOTI (PEARL)

Pearl is of planet Moon. Person with weak Moon and person with Cancer at his Rashi should wear pearl.

Method of wearing: Pearl should be between 3¼ to 9¼ Ratti. Pearl fixed in silver may be worn in neck, arm or on Sun finger of right hand in the case of male and left hand in case of female. The day to wear the pearl for the first time is Monday evening, just after Sun-set, during the bright fortnight.

MANTRA FOR WEARING PEARL

Recite the following Mantra 11 times by holding pearl in your hand and wear.

Aum Emam Devaa Asa-pathnam Suvadhwam Mahathe
Kshethraaya Mahathe Jyeshtaaya Mahathe Jaana
Rajyaayendra Syendri-yaaya, Emam Manushya Putra
Mamushi Putra Mamushie Puthra-Mashie Visham
Eva Vodasee Raajaa Sowmosmaakam
Braahamanaanaam Raaja.

MOONGA (CORAL)

Coral is of the planet Mars. Person with Aries or Scorpio as his Rashi and if Mars is weak in his horoscope should wear coral.

METHOD OF WEARING

Coral between 6¼ to 25¼ Ratti weight fixed in Gold may be worn. If Mars and Moon are placed together in a horoscope, Coral may be fixed in silver or copper. The day to wear Coral is Tuesday one hour after sun-rise. Wear it on the right hand Sun finger or arm or in the neck.

MANTRA FOR WEARING

Aum Agnimoordhaa Diva: Kakuthpathi:
Prthivyaa Ayam. Apaam Rethaamsi Jinwathi.

PANNA (EMERALD)

Panna is of the planet mercury. Person with Gemini or Virgo Rashi and if Mercury is weak in a horoscope, should wear emerald.

METHOD OF WEARING

Emerald between 4¼ to 11¼ Ratti may be fixed in gold and worn on the 5th, 14th or 23rd of the birth month or on any Wednesday just after two hours of Sunrise. This may be worn in neck, right arm or on the finger of mercury in the right hand.

MANTRA FOR WEARING

Recite the following Mantra 11 times by holding Emerald in your hand and wear.

AUM Ud-Budhya-Swaathane Prathi
Jaagra-hithwa Mishtaa-Pootha
Samsa-je-yaa-mayam Cha.

Asmitha-sathe Adhyuthara-swin Viswadevaa
Yajamaana-sarcha See-de-ttha.

PUKHRAJ (YELLOW SAPPHIRE)

Yellow Sapphire is of the planet Jupiter. Person with Sagittarius or Pisces Rashi and if Jupiter is weak in one's horoscope, should wear yellow sapphire.

METHOD OF WEARING

Yellow Sapphire may be fixed in gold ring. The quality should be fine weighing 5¼ to 18¼ Ratti. Wear it on Thursday just before one hour of Sunset. It may be worn in neck, right arm or on Sun finger of right arm. The weight of Yellow Sapphire should be minimum 3 Rattis.

MANTRA FOR WEARING

Recite the following Mantra for 11 times by holding yellow sapphire in your hand. However, you can recite any number of times. The more the number of time is recitation the more will be the result.

AUM Brahaspthe Athio Yadiryo
Arhaadhya-madhi-bhaathi Krathumajjneshu.

Yadhee-daye-chavasha Rtha-prajaatha Tadas-maasu
Dwivinam Dhehi Chitram

HEERA (DIAMOND)

Diamond is of the planet Venus. Person with Taurus or Libra Rashi or if Venus is weak in horoscope, should wear a diamond.

METHOD OF WEARING

Diamond may be fixed in gold, silver or in white metal ring and worn on Friday morning.

MANTRA FOR WEARING

Recite the following Mantra for 11 times by holding Heera (Diamond) in your hand.

AUM Annaathu Paris-thruthom Rasam Brahmanaa
Vyapivath Kshatram Paya: Somam Prajaapitha: Rthene
Sathya-mindriyam Vipaanam Shukra-mandhasa
Endrasye-endriya-midam Payomritham Madhu.

NEELAM (BLUE SAPPHIRE)

Blue Sapphire is of the planet Saturn. Person with Capricorn or Aquarius Rashi should wear Blue Sapphire. Blue Sapphire can also be worn during the dasa of Saturn.

METHOD OF WEARING

5¼ to 10¼ Ratti Sapphire may be fixed in eight-metal ring on Saturday two hours before Sunrise. Before wearing it permanently, keep this in black coloured cloth and wear it on arm for three days. If the results are favourable this can be worn on the Saturn finger.

MANTRA FOR WEARING

Recite the following Mantra 11 times by holding Blue Sapphire in your hands.

Aum Sanno Deveera-bhishtaya Aapo Bhavanthu,
Peethaye Shamyo Rabhistra-vanthu Na:

GOMED (ZIRCON)

Gomed is of shadowy planet Rahu. This may be worn during the dasa of Rahu.

METHOD OF WEARING

Gomed should be between 7¼ to 24¼ Ratti. Wear this in the evening or two hours after Sunrise on Wednesday on Saturday.

MANTRA FOR WEARING

Recite the following Mantra for 11 times by holding Gomed in your hand.

AUM Kayaana-shi-chatra Aabhuva Doothi Sadda Vrdha: Sakhaa Kayaa Shachish-tayaa Vrthaa.

LAHSUNIYA (CAT'S EYE)

Cat's eye is of the shadowy Planet Ketu. It may be worn during the dasa of Ketu.

METHOD OF WEARING

Cat's eye should be between 3¼ to 8¼ Ratti. This may be fixed in silver ring and worn during mid-night on ring finger.

MANTRA FOR WEARING

Recite the following Mantra 11 times by holding Cat's eye in your hand and wear.

AUM Kethum Krpa-vanna Kethave Pesho-maryyaa Apeshas. Samu-shadwiraa-jaayathaa.

MANTRAS
TO CONTROL HEADACHE
(1)

Aum namo Arahanthaanam, Aum Namo Siddhaanam,

Aum Namo Aayariyaanam, Aum Namo Uvajhaayaanam,

Aum Namo Loye Savva-saahoonam.

Aum Namo, Aum Namo Naanaaya, Aum Namo Damsanaaya,

Aum Namo Charithaaya, Aum Namo Trhilokya-vasyamkari

Hrim Swaaha.

Direction	:	North
Day	:	Any day
Recitation	:	7 Malas
Dress	:	Yellow
Mala	:	Tulsi
Asan	:	Cotton

(Keep Bowl full of water and recite the Mantra. Look deep into the water for purification. Give the holy water to the patient)

TO CONTROL TEMPERATURE
(2)

Aum Hrin Namo Loye Savva-saahoonam;
Aum Hrin Namo Uvajhaanam;
Aum Hrin Namo Aayariyaanam;
Aum Hrin Namo Siddhaanam;
Aum Hrin Namo Arahanthaanam.

Direction	:	North
Day	:	Any day
Recitation	:	7 Malas
Dress	:	Yellow
Mala	:	Tulsi
Asan	:	Cotton

(Keep bowl full of water and recite the Mantra. Look deep into the water for purification. Give this holy water to the patient)

TO RELEASE FROM JAIL
(3)

Nam-husaava Vrsaelo Monn.
Namya-jhaajyau Monn.
Nam-yaari-eaa Monn.
Nam-dwassi Monn.
Namtha-hamraa Monn.

Direction	:	West
Day	:	Any day
Recitation	:	7 Malas for 21 days
Mala	:	Pearl/Coral
Asan	:	Cotton Black

(Prisoner can recite the Mantra under the instructions of Sadhak/Guru)

TO HARM A THIEF
(4)

Aum Namo Arahanthaanam Dhanu Dhanu Mahaadhanu Mahaadhanu Swaahaa.

Direction	:	South
Day	:	Any day
Recitation	:	1.25 Lac
Dress	:	Black
Mala	:	Baheda
Asan	:	Lion's skin
Deity	:	Before Kali Ma

TO CONTROL FEAR OF
GHOST / ENEMIES
(5)

Aum Hrin A-Si-Aa-U-Sa Sarva Dushtaana
Sthambhaya-Sthambhaya Mohaya-Mohaya
Andhaya-Andhaya Mookvath-Kaaraya Kuru
Kuru Hrin Dushtaana To: ta: Ta:.

Direction	:	South
Day	:	Any day
Recitation	:	108 times in morning for 21 days.
Dress	:	White
Mala	:	Rudraksh
Asan	:	Black
Place	:	Before Durga between 6:00 p.m. to 8:00 p.m.

FOR VICTORY IN DEBATES
(6)

**Aum Hran Sa: Aum Arham Ayen
Sreem A-Si-Aa-U-Sa Nameh.**

Direction	:	East
Day	:	Wednesday
Recitation	:	2.25 Lac
Dress	:	White
Mala	:	Green Stone
Asan	:	White
Deity	:	Sarswati Ma
Time	:	8.00 a.m.

TO ATTAIN KNOWLEDGE AND VICTORY IN DEBATES
(7)

Aum Hrin A-Si-Aa-U-Sa Namo Arham
Vada Vada Vaag vaadinee Sathya Vaadini
Vada Vada Mama Vakthrem Vyaktha
Vaajayaahreem Sathyam-Broohi Sathyam
Broohi Sathyam Vada Sathyam Vada
Askhalitha Prajaaram Sadaiva Manujaa
Surasadasi Hrin Arham A-Si-Aa-U-Saa Nameh

Direction	:	East
Day	:	Wednesday
Recitation	:	108 times for 90 days
Dress	:	White
Mala	:	Green Stone
Asan	:	White
Deity	:	Ma Saraswati
Time	:	8.00 a.m.

FOR SUCCESS IN FOREIGN TRAVEL
(8)

Aum Namo Arahanthaanam, Aum Namo Bhaga-
vayiya
Chantaa-Yayi-ye-Satha-ttaaye-Gire Mor Mor Hulu
Hulu Chulu Chulu Mayur Vahiniye Swaahaa.

Direction	:	East
Day	:	Monday
Recitation	:	108 times for 41 days
Dress	:	White
Mala	:	Pearl
Asan	:	Cotton cloth of 7 colours
Deity	:	Lord Shiva
Time	:	9.00 a.m. to 10.00 a.m.

TO OVERCOME ANXIETY AND FULFILL DESIRES
(9)

Aum Hran Hrim Hrown Hra:
A-Si-Aa-U-Saa Nama: Swaahaa:

Direction	:	East
Day	:	Thursday
Recitation	:	108 times for 90 days
Dress	:	Yellow
Mala	:	Rudraksha
Asan	:	Mrigchala
Deity	:	Your Own Guru
Time	:	Before 8.00 a.m.

TO ATTAIN WEALTH
(10)

Arahantha, Siddha, Aariya, Uvajham,
Savva-Saahoonam.

Direction	:	West
Day	:	Sunday
Recitation	:	1.25 Lac
Dress	:	White
Mala	:	Chandan
Asan	:	Mrigchala
Deity	:	Lakshmi
Time	:	Between 4.00 a.m. to 6.00 a.m.

FOR NAME, FAME AND WEALTH
(11)

Aum Namo Arahanthaanam, Aum Namo Siddhaanam,
Aum Namo Aayariyaanam, Aum Namo Uvajhaayaanam,
Aum Namo Loye Savva-Sahoonam.
Aum Hrim Hrom Hrowm Hra: Nama: Swaahaa.

Direction	:	West
Day	:	Sunday
Recitation	:	3.25 Lac
Dress	:	Yellow
Mala	:	Rudraksh
Asan	:	Mrigchala
Deity	:	Lakshmi
Time	:	6.00 a.m. to 8.00 a.m.

FOR POSSESSIONS OF ALL ARTS
(12)

Aum Hrin Srin Araham A Si Aa U Saa Namah

Direction	:	East
Day	:	Wednesday
Recitation	:	1.25 Lac
Dress	:	White
Mala	:	Emerald or Green Stone
Asan	:	Multi-colour cotton cloth
Deity	:	Lord Shiva
Time	:	Before 8.00 a.m.

WEALTH AND FULFILLMENT OF DESIRES
(13)

Aum Arahanthanam, Siddhaanam Aayariyaanam Uvvajhaayaanam Saahoonam Mama Ridhim Vriddhim Sameehitham Kuru Kuru Swaahaa.

Direction	:	East
Day	:	Thursday
Recitation	:	11 Malas for 41 days, morning and evening after taking bath
Dress	:	Pure silk white
Mala	:	Rudraksh
Asan	:	Mrigchala
Deity	:	Lord Vishnu or your own guru

(Results will be 10 times if Sadhna is done on the bank of river)

FOR MALE CHILD
(14)

Aum Hrin Srin Klim Hrin Asi Aausaa Chulu Chulu
Hulu Hulu Mulu Mulu Echiyam Me Kuru Kuru
Swaahaa.
Thribbhuvana swamino Vidya.

Direction	:	East
Day	:	Thursday
Recitation	:	11 Malas for 90 days. Offer one white flower to lord Krishna after every Mala.
Dress	:	Pure Silk white/cream
Mala	:	Pearl or Rudraksh
Asan	:	Mrigchala

(Immerse 108 white pearls in the flowing water after completion)

TO CONTROL MINISTER / V.I.P.
(15)

Aum Hrin Namo Arahanthaanam, Aum Hrin Namo Siddhaanam. Aum Hrim Namo Aayariyaanam. Aum
Hrin Namo Uvayhaayaanam. Aum Hrin Namo Loye
Savva-Sahoonam. Amukam Mama Vashyam Kuru Kuru. Vashat.

Direction	:	East
Day	:	Friday
Recitation	:	21 Malas
Dress	:	Yellow
Mala	:	Rudraksh
Asan	:	Cotton

Recite the name of the person in place of (Amuk). After completion put one Elaichi from the mala in your mouth while meeting the minister/V.I.P.

FOR VASHIKARAN
(16)

Aum Namo Arahanthaanam. Are (Aari)
Ar (Ari) Namohinll Amukam Moha
Mohay Swaahaa.

Direction	:	East
Day	:	Friday
Recitation	:	108 times for 41 days
Dress	:	White
Mala	:	Chotti Elaichi
Asan	:	Cotton

(Recite the name of the person in place of (Amuk). After completion of Mantra offer one elaichi from the mala to the person concerned).

TO OVERCOME FEAR FROM SNAKES
(17)

Aum Araham A Si Aa U Saa Anaahath Jayi Arham Nama:

Direction	:	North
Day	:	Monday
Recitation	:	108 times for 40 days
Dress	:	Multi colour
Mala	:	Chandan (Try to make use of fingers)
Asan	:	Mrigchala
Deity	:	Lord Shiva

(You will not have fear of snakes throughout the life if the Mantra is recited on the day of Diwali, Suraya Grehan or Chandar Grehan).

PROTECTION FROM ENEMIES
(18)

Aum Arham Amukam Dushtam Saadhaya Saadhya A Si Aa U Saa Nama:

Direction	:	South
Day	:	Saturday
Recitation	:	108 times for 41 days
Dress	:	Black
Mala	:	Beheda
Asan	:	Black
Deity	:	Bhairon

(Recite the name of enemy in place of Amuk)

TO GAIN WEALTH
(19)

Aum Hrin Hrun Namo Arahanthaanam Hrun Nameh.

Direction	:	West
Day	:	Sunday
Recitation	:	1.25 Lac
Dress	:	White
Mala	:	Chandan
Deity	:	Lakshmi
Asan	:	Mrigchala
Time	:	Between 4.00 a.m. to 6.00 a.m.

TO CURE DISEASE
(20)

Aum Namo Savvo Sahi Patthaanam.
Aum Namo Khelo Sahi Patthaanam.
Aum Namo Sallo Sahi Patthaanam.
Aum Namo Savvo Sahi Patthaanam.
Aum Aem Hrin Sreen Kleem Klomn
Arham Nama.

Direction	:	North
Day	:	Tuesday
Recitation	:	108 times daily for 21 days
Dress	:	Yellow
Mala	:	Rudraksh
Asan	:	Mrigchala
Deity	:	Your own God/Goddess
Time	:	Before 10.00 a.m.

FOR BUSINESS AND PROSPERITY
(21)

Aum Hrin Srin Araham Asi Aa U Saa Anahatha-Vidheyam Araham Nama:

Direction	:	West
Day	:	Thursday
Dress	:	Yellow
Asan	:	Yellow cotton
Deity	:	Durga
Time	:	Before 8.00 a.m. and in evening between 7.00 p.m. and 8.00 p.m.

TO OVERCOME FEAR
(22)

Aum Namo Saddhaanam Panchenam.

Direction	:	North
Day	:	Monday
Recitation	:	108 times for 40 days
Dress	:	Multi-colour
Mala	:	Chandan (Try to make use of fingers)
Asan	:	Mrigchala
Deity	:	Lord Shiva

(You will not have fear throughout the life if the Mantra is recited on the day of Diwali, Suraya, Grehan or Chander Grehan.)

TO CURE ALL DISEASES
(23)

Aum Ayen Hrin Klin Klon Klon Araham Nameh:

Direction	:	North
Day	:	Tuesday
Recitation	:	Before 8.00 a.m. and at night before sleeping.
Mala	:	Mala of cloves for 108 times
Asan	:	Cotton
Deity	:	Lord Shiva

TO ACHIEVE ALL ROUND SUCCESS
(24)

Aum Arahantha Siddha Aayariya Uvajhaaya
Savva-Saahoo, Sava Dhammathi Thyaraanam
Aum Namo Bhagavayeea Suyadevayaaye
Shaanthi Devayanam Sarva Pavaayanam
Devayaanam Dasaanam Disaa Paalaanam
Panchloka Paalaanam.
Aum Hrin Arahantha Devam Nama :
Sree Sarva Jumooham Kuru Kuru Swaahaa:

Direction	:	West
Day	:	Thursday
Recitation	:	Seven Mala per day before 8.00 a.m.
Mala	:	Rudraksh
Asan	:	Mrigchala
Deity	:	Your own Guru

FOR SELF-PROTECTION
(25)

Patamam Havayie Mangalam Brajamayi Shilaa-masthakopari
Namo Arahanthaanam Angushta Yo: Namo
Siddhanam Tarjanyo: Namo Aayariyaanam
Madhyamayo: Namo Uvajhaayaanam Anaamikayo:
Namo Loye-Savva-Sahoonam Kanishtakayo : Iso
Pancha Namo-Yaaro Bcrajamayi Praakaaram,
Savva-paavappanaasane Jala-brthara Vaathikaa,
Mangalaanam Cha Savvessim Khaadirangaara-Poorna Khaathikaa.

Direction	:	North
Day	:	Tuesday
Recitation	:	Just count on fingers 108 times at night
Asan	:	Black sheet on your bed
Deity	:	Lord Shiva

TO REMOVE FEAR OF THIEF
(26)

Aum Namo Arihanthaanam
Aamiranee Mohanee
Mohaya Mohaya Swaahaa.

Just count on fingers for 108 times
irrespective of any religious code,
time, direction, asan and surroundings.

TO FULFILL DESIRES
(27)

Aum Hrin A Si Aa U Saa Nameh: (Maha Mantra-
Supreme Mantra)
A Si Aa U Saa Nameh (Mula Mantra-root Mantra)
Aum Hrin Arhathe Utpthe Swaahaa (Thribuvana
Mantra)

Direction	:	East
Day	:	Thursday
Recitation	:	108 times before 8.00 a.m.
Mala	:	Lotus
Asan	:	Multi coloured cloth
Deity	:	Lord Shiva

TO CONTROL THE NINE PLANETS
(28)

Aum Namo Arahanthaanam Hran Swaahaa.
Aum Namo Siddhaanam Hrin Swaahaa.
Aum Namo Aayariyaanam Hrum Swaahaa.
Aum Namo Uvajhaayaanam Hron Swaahaa.
Aum Namo Loye-Savva-Sahoonam Hra: Swaahaa.

Direction	:	East
Day	:	Monday
Recitation	:	108 times before Sunrise
Mala	:	Chandan
Asan	:	Mrigchala
Deity	:	Lord Shiva

Remarks : Chanting of Mantra is 1000 times auspicious during lunar or solar eclipse.

FOR OVER-ALL PROSPERITY
(29)

Samyak-darshana Jnana Chaarithraaya Nama:

Direction	:	East
Day	:	Thursday
Recitation	:	108 times before 8.00 a.m.
Mala	:	Lotus
Asan	:	Multi coloured cotton
Deity	:	Lord Shiva

FOR OVER-ALL PROSPERITY
(30)

Aum Hran Hrim Hrom Hrowm Hra:
A-Si-Aa-U-Saa-Sarva Shanti
Thushtim Pushtiṃ Kuru Kuru
Swaahaa. Aum Hrim Araham Nama:
Kleem Srvaarogyam Kuru Kuru Swaahaa.

Direction	:	East
Day	:	Monday
Recitation	:	108 times before sunrise
Mala	:	Chandan
Asan	:	Mrigchala
Deity	:	Lord Shiva

Remarks: Chanting of Mantra is 1000 times auspicious during lunar or solar eclipse.

TO ATTAIN WEALTH
(31)

Aum Hrim A-Si-Aa-U-Saa Hrim Namah

Direction	:	West
Day	:	Sunday
Recitation	:	1.25 Lac
Dress	:	White
Mala	:	Chandan
Asan	:	Mrigchala
Deity	:	Lakshmi
Time	:	Between 4.00 a.m. and 6.00 a.m.

FOR FULFILLMENT OF DESIRES
(32)

Aum Klin Hrin Hrain Aem Hrim
(Hran Hrin) Hra: Aparaajithaayai
Namah.

Direction	:	East
Day	:	Thursday
Recitation	:	11 Malas for 41 days in morning and evening after taking bath.
Dress	:	Pure silk white
Mala	:	Rudraksh
Asan	:	Mrigchala
Deity	:	Lord Vishnu or your own Guru

(Results will be 10 times if Sadhana is done on the bank of the river).

TO OVERCOME SERVICE PROBLEMS
(33)

Aum Paarshwanaathya Hrin.

Direction   :   West

Day   :   Thursday

Recitation   :   101 Malas daily for 11 days

Dress   :   Yellow

Mala   :   Mala of crystals

Asan   :   Cotton

(Observe all religious codes and sleep on floor)

FOR REMOVAL OF FEAR
(34)

Aum Aam Hran Kshweem Aum Hrin.

Direction	:	East
Day	:	Monday
Recitation	:	11 malas daily for 41 days
Mala	:	Rudraksh
Asan	:	Black Cotton

TO OVERCOME FEAR
(35)

Aum Hrin Srin Kali Kundadandaaya Hrin Namah.

Direction	:	East
Day	:	Monday
Recitation	:	11 malas daily for 41 days
Mala	:	Rudraksh
Asan	:	Black cotton

FOR BLESSINGS OF YOUR DEITY
(36)

Aum Aam Kron hrin aem klim hron padmaavathayai Nameh.

Direction	:	East
Day	:	Tuesday
Recitation	:	101 mala daily between 6 p.m. to 10.00 p.m.
Dress	:	White
Mala	:	Rudraksh or red pearl
Asan	:	White
Place	:	Bank of river or place of worship

Adopt all religious codes and brahmcharya and sleep on floor. God will appear in your dreams.

TO INCREASE MEMORY
(37)

Aum Aem Srin Klin Vad Vad Vaagvaadinee Hrim Saraswathayya Nameh

Aum Jhrown Jhrown Shudha Budhi pradehi sruth-devee-Mar-hathham thubhyam Nameh.

Direction	:	North
Day	:	Tuesday
Recitation	:	Before 8.00 a.m. and at night before sleeping.
Mala	:	Mala of cloves for 108 times.
Asan	:	Cotton
Deity	:	Lord Shiva

TO INCREASE INTUTION POWER
(38)

Aum Hrin Laam Hram Pa Lakshmim Jweem
Kshweem Ku: Hamsa: Swaaha.

Direction	:	East
Day	:	Wednesday
Recitation	:	1.25 Lac
Dress	:	White
Mala	:	Emrald or green stone
Asan	:	Multi colour cotton cloth
Deity	:	Lord Shiva
Time	:	Before 8.00 a.m.

Sadhak should sit before the Deity while reciting mantra.

Adopt all religious code and sleep on floor till Almighty whispers
in your ear the same.

TO INCREASE HEALING POWER
(39)

Aum Hrin La Hran Pa Lakshmi
Hamsa: Swaahaa.

Direction	:	East
Day	:	Thursday
Recitation	:	11 Malas for 41 days in morning and evening after taking bath.
Dress	:	Pure silk white
Mala	:	Rudraksh
Asan	:	Mrigchala
Deity	:	Lord Vishnu or your own Guru

You will attain mantra sidhi. You can remove any kind of poison simply by touching the person affected with poison. Recite 21 times simultaneously by touching.

FOR RELIEF FROM CRIMINAL CASES
(40)

Aum Rshabhaaya Nameh:

OR

Aum Hrin Srin Klim Chakresvari Mama
Raksham Kuru Kuru Swaaha.

Direction	:	East
Day	:	Thursday
Recitation	:	11 malas for 41 days in morning and evening after taking bath.
Dress	:	Pure silk white
Mala	:	Rudraksh
Asan	:	Mrigchala
Deity	:	Lord Vishnu or your own guru

You will see in your dreams all auspicious and happy things.

FOR INFATUATION
(41)

AUM Nameh Bhagavao Arahao Pushpadamthassa Sijjashyao Mem Bhagavaye Mahayi Mahaavidya Puffa, Mahapuffe, Puffasue Ta: Ta: Ta: Swahaa.

Direction	:	East
Day	:	Thursday
Recitation	:	108 times for 90 days
Dress	:	Yellow
Mala	:	Rudraksh
Asan	:	Mrigchala
Deity	:	Your own Guru
Time	:	Before 8.00 a.m.

Recite the Mantra by holding a fruit or flower in your hand. Keep fast for two days before the commencement of recitation. If you give the fruit or flower to any person after reciting the Mantra for further 21 times, He/she will be infatuated.

FOR TREATMENT OF EYES
(42)

Aum Nameh Bhagavao Arahao Sivalajinassa
Sijjashyao Mem
Bhagavayi Mahayi Mahaavidyaa Soyale Soyale
Paseeyale Pasanthi
Nivvuaa Nivvaana Nivvuyethi Nameh Bhavathi
Ta: Ta: Ta: Swahaa.

Direction	:	North
Day	:	Any day
Recitation	:	7 Malas
Dress	:	Yellow
Mala	:	Tulsi
Asan	:	Cotton

Keep a bowl full of water and recite the Mantra. Look deep
into the water for purification. Diseases of eyes, head etc. can
be cured by washing with the holy water for 11 times.

TO OVERCOME GHOST
(43)

Aum Nameh Bhagavao Arahao Sindhyaam-sassa
Sijjhashyao Mem bhagavayi Mahayi Mahaavidhyaa
Sijjase Sijjase eyam Kre Mahaaseyam Kare
Pabbham
Kare Suppabham Kare Ta: Swahaa.

Recite the above Mantra by holding
flowers during night. Keep fast for
two days before the commencement of
the recitation. Pass the flower so
purified with the Mantra over the body
of a person affected with the ghost or
any disease which cannot be diagnosed.
There will be complete relief.

TO OVERCOME DEADLY DISEASES
(44)

Aum Nameh Bhagavao Arahao Kum Thussa
Sijjashyao Me Bhagavayi Mahayi Mahaavidyaa
Kum Thude Kum The Kum Thumayi Ta: Ta: Ta:
Aum Kum Theshwar Kum The Swaahaa.

Direction	:	North
Day	:	Monday
Recitation	:	108 times for 40 days
Dress	:	Multi colour
Mala	:	Chandan (Try to make use of fingers)
Asan	:	Mrigchala
Deity	:	Lord Shiva

Take ash and water from a graveyard and put it in a bowl.
Look deep into the water for purification while doing Pooja.
Put the ash and water on the floor where persons with contagious
or deadly diseases are staying.

MANTRA FOR VASHIKARAN
(45)

Aum Namah Bhagavao Arahao Mallissa Sijjashyao
Mem Bhagavayi Mahayi Mahaavidyaa Mallisu
Malli
Jaya Mallipadi Malli Ta: Ta: Ta: Swahaa.

Direction	:	East
Day	:	Thursday
Recitation	:	11 Malas for 41 days in morning and evening after taking bath
Dress	:	Pure silk white
Mala	:	Rudraksh
Asan	:	Mrigchala
Deity	:	Lord Vishnu or your own guru

Purify a piece of garment and the Mala with the above Mantra
and give to the person whom you want to bring closer to you.
He/She will come to you.

SARV SIDDHI MANTRA
(46)

Mahamaritanjye Mantra is the most auspicious Mantra in the Vedas. Daily recitation of this Mantra is very useful to the Sadhaka and saves and helps man in the many difficulties and hurdles of life. It is tested Mantra.

**Aum Hung Jung aum Bhoorbhava Swaha:
Aum Tryamakam Yajamaha Saugandhim
Pushtivardhanam Diyoyona Prachodayat
Urvarukmev Bandhananmrityomu mamritamat
Swaha
Bhoova Bhooh Aum Sah Joon Houng Aum.**

Direction	:	East
Day	:	Thursday
Recitation	:	11 Malas for 41 days in Morning and evening after taking bath.
Dress	:	Pure silk white
Mala	:	Rudraksh
Asan	:	Mrigchala
Deity	:	Lord Vishnu or your own Guru

SARV SIDDHI MANTRA
(47)

Aum Hoong Sah Aum Boorbhava Swaha Aum
Tarayambakam yajyamaha Aum Tasyavitru
Varaneyam Aum sugandhim Pushtivardhanam
Aum Bhargo Devasya Dhimahi Aum Urava-
arukmev
Bandhnat Aum Diyo yo na Prachodyat Aum
Mritiyomukshye Mamritat Aum Swaha Bhoova
Bhoo Aum Sah Joon Hoong Aum.

Direction	:	East
Day	:	Thursday
Recitation	:	11 Malas for 41 days in Morning and evening after taking bath.
Dress	:	Pure silk white
Mala	:	Rudraksh
Asan	:	Mrigchala
Deity	:	Lord Vishnu or your own Guru

FOR EDUCATION
(48)

Another strong Mantra for education, intelligence and wealth is given below. This must be recited one lakh times.

Aum Krin Krin Krin
Or
Aum sacheda Keem Bhram
Hareeng Sachedakanek Bhram
Or
Aum Sacheda Keemam Bhram

Direction	:	East
Day	:	Wednesday
Recitation	:	2.25 lac
Dress	:	White
Mala	:	Green Stone
Asan	:	White
Deity	:	Sarswati Ma
Time	:	8.00 a.m.

(One mala of the above Mantra should be recited daily for 41 days).

FOR ATTAINING MOKSHA
(49)

To attain Moksha, One should recite one Mala of the following Mantras daily. These are very powerful Mantras.

Aum Namo Bhagwate Sarv Bhut Atmaney Varrivaye

Or

Sarv Atam Sanyog Yogpadam Pith Atmaney Nameh

Or

Aum Shree Hrin Krin Krishnaye Swaha:

Direction	:	North
Day	:	Tuesday
Recitation	:	Just count on fingers 108 times at night
Asan	:	Black sheet on your bed
Deity	:	Lord Shiva

LAKSHMI MANTRA
(50)

Recite the Mantra one lack times five times daily. One is blessed with wealth. This is a tested Mantra.

Aum Namo Dhandaye Swaha

The same Mantra holds good for
Shri Vidya and Bhuvneswari as these
are the other names of the Goddess
with which she is known in other
parts of the country.

The Mantra bestows happiness
and is also recited in case of
troubles and turmoils.

FOR SUCCESS IN ELECTION
(51)

To achieve all the political objectives one should recite any one of the following Mantras with full confidence 21 times a day for 90 days. One will be crowned with success and occupy high office as a minister etc.

Aum emminder Vardhaye shteriyame
ma emam Vishmek virsham Kirinu Tawam
Nirmitranakshanu Hasye Sarvastan Randyasam
Ahmutrashu

OR

Aayemastu Dhanpatidharnanabhayme Visham
Vishwpatirastu Raja Asminndera Mahi Varcharsi
Ghehavchasam Krinuhi Shatrubhasam.

OR

Yunijam ta uttravantminder Yana Jayanti na Prajat Te,
Yastavam Kardekvarsham Jananmutam Manpanam

Direction	:	East
Day	:	Wednesday
Recitation	:	2.25 lac
Dress	:	White
Mala	:	Green stone
Asan	:	White
Deity	:	Sarswati Ma
Time	:	8.00 a.m.

FOR YASH PRAPTI
(52)

By the Japa of this Mantra all people will be indebted to you. You will be respected and others will acknowledge the good done to them. This mantra must be recited 21 times a day for 90 days continuously.

Aum giravargrateshu Hirnye ch goshu cha.
Suryam Sicheymanayam kekale mandhu Tanmeye

Direction	:	East
Day	:	Thursday
Recitation	:	11 Malas for 41 days in morning and evening after taking bath.
Dress	:	Pure silk white
Mala	:	Rudraksh
Asan	:	Mrigchala
Deity	:	Lord Vishnu or your own guru

FOR HAVING PROGENY
(53)

In case the couple does not have a child, one can acquire progeny through Mantras, provided one does the Sadhana with full faith following the prescribed rituals.

AUM Shri Hrin Klin Glin

Or

Aum Devekisut Govind Vasudev Jagatpite Dehi ye Taney Krishna Tawamahem Sharanam Gata

Direction	:	East
Day	:	Thursday
Dress	:	Pure silk white/cream
Mala	:	Pearl or Rudraksh
Asan	:	Mrigchala

(The Mantra should be recited 3 lakh times continuously).

KRODH SHANTI MANTRA
(54)

This Mantra controls one's anger.
When one suffers due to anger
this Mantra should be recited.

Aum Shante Parshante Sarv Krodh Pashnon Swaha

Direction   :   East

Day   :   Any day

Recitation   :   Five minutes

(Fold your hand and close your eyes).

FOR SUCCESSFUL COMPLETION OF ALL JOBS
(55)

It must be recited 11,000 times to obtain Sidhi of the Mantra. When you are to start any work or have a meeting with any important man for some specific work etc. recite the Mantra 108 times. You will succeed in obtaining your goal. The Mantra reads as:

Aum Nameh sarvarthsadhni Swaha:

Direction   :   West

Day   :   Thursday

Recitation   :   7 Malas in a day before 8.00 a.m.

Mala   :   Rudraksh

Asan   :   Mrigchala

Deity   :   Your own Guru

TO ATTRACT ALL OR ANYONE
(56)

This mantra is called "SARV AAKARSHAN MANTRA".

Aum Chamunde Tarutatu Amukaye
akarshaye Akarshaye Swaha:

Recite the mantra one thousand times daily for 21 days. Replace
the name of the person in place of the word "AMUK". One
will be infatuated. Every male or female can use this mantra.

Direction	:	East
Day	:	Thursday
Dress	:	Yellow
Mala	:	Rudraksha
Asan	:	Mrigchala
Deity	:	Your own Guru
Time	:	Before 8.00 a.m.

FOR SUCCESS IN DEBATES
(57)

Aum Namo Namo Patheya Budhaanam

Direction	:	East
Day	:	Wednesday
Recitation	:	2.25 lac
Dress	:	White
Mala	:	Green stone
Asan	:	White
Deity	:	Sarswati Ma
Time	:	8.00 a.m.

TO CURE
MENSTRUAL TROUBLE
(58)

Aum Tadyathaa Garbhadhara Dhaarinee
Garbha-rakshinee aakaasha Maathriki Hum
Phat Swaahaa.

Direction	:	North
Day	:	Monday
Recitation	:	108 times for 40 days
Dress	:	Multi colour
Mala	:	Chandan (Try to make use of fingers)
Asan	:	Mrigchala
Deity	:	Lord Shiva

FOR PROSPERITY
(59)

Aum Hraam Hrim Hroom Hrowm Hra:
Asi Aa-u-saa asya
Devadattam naamadheyasyya Mana: Pushtim
Kuru Do Swaha

Direction	:	East
Day	:	Thursday
Recitation	:	108 times before 8.00 a.m.
Mala	:	Lotus
Asan	:	Multi-coloured cotton
Deity	:	Lord Shiva

Recite the name of the Sadhaka in place of Devadattam.

FOR PROSPERITY
(60)

Aum Hrim Hrim Srim Klim Bloom Kalikunda Danda Swamina Siddhim Jagadwasam Aanaya Aanaya Swaahaa.

Direction	:	East
Day	:	Thursday
Recitation	:	108 times before 8.00 a.m.
Mala	:	Lotus
Asan	:	Multi-coloured cotton
Deity	:	Lord Shiva

FOR FULFILLMENT OF DESIRE
(61)

Take Mustard Seeds (Sarso) and recite the following Mantra for 108 times. Keep these seeds in your hands when going to important work. All your desires will be fulfilled.

Aum Purushakaaye Aghoraaye Pravega Tho Jaaya Lahu Kuru-Kuru Swaahaa.

Direction	:	East
Day	:	Thursday
Recitation	:	108 times before 8.00 a.m.
Asan	:	Multi-coloured cloth
Deity	:	Lord Shiva

MANTRA FOR INFATUATION
(62)

Aum Namo Bhagavavo Abhinadnansya Sijhashyao
Me Bhagavayi Mahayi Mahavidhya-nandane
Abhi-nandhane Ta: Ta: Ta: Swaahaa

Direction	:	East
Day	:	Thursday
Recitation	:	108 times for 90 days
Dress	:	Yellow
Mala	:	Rudraksha
Asan	:	Mrigchala
Deity	:	Your own Guru
Time	:	Before 8.00 a.m.

MANTRA FOR SUCCESSFUL
ACTOR / ARTIST
(63)

Aum Namo Sayam Budhinam
Jhrowm Jhrowm Swaahaa

Direction	:	East
Day	:	Thursday
Recitation	:	108 times before 8.00 a.m.
Mala	:	Lotus
Asan	:	Multi-coloured cotton
Deity	:	Lord Shiva

(Recite the Mantra after bath).

MANTRA TO CONTROL EPILEPSY
(64)

Aum Namo Jalo Sahi-patthaanam.

Take water from holy place and recite the following Mantra for 1100 times. Give this water to the person suffering from epilepsy.

Direction	:	North
Day	:	Any day
Dress	:	Yellow
Mala	:	Tulsi
Asan	:	Cotton

FOR SUCCESS IN WORK
(65)

Aum Purushakaaye Aghoraaye Pravega
Tho Jaaya Lahu Kuru Kuru Swaahaa.

Take mustard seeds (Sarson) and recite the following Mantra for 108 times. Keep these seeds in your hand when going to important work. All your desires will be fulfilled.

Direction	:	East
Day	:	Monday
Recitation	:	108 times
Dress	:	White
Asan	:	Cotton cloth of seven colours
Deity	:	Lord Shiva
Time	:	9.00 a.m. to 10.00 a.m.

SAI MUSIC MANDIR

The One Shop for Shopping

If you wish to Receive weekly News Letter from us Regarding New
Releasese, Please E-mail us at musicmandir@yahoo.com

We are Dealing with : **Instrumental Music**

- ☐ Carnatic Music
- ☐ Hindustani Music
- ☐ Bhajans
- ☐ Ghazals
- ☐ Old Hits
- ☐ Ramayana DVD
- ☐ Krishna DVD
- ☐ Mahabarata DVD
- ☐ Sai Bhajans
- ☐ Om Namashivaya DVD etc..

Music Instruments

- ☐ Tabla
- ☐ Harmonium
- ☐ Sitar
- ☐ Dholak
- ☐ Naal
- ☐ Flute
- ☐ Tambura
- ☐ Veena etc....

Handicrafts

- ☐ Statues
- ☐ Woodencarvings
- ☐ Paintings
- ☐ Photographs
- ☐ Gift Items Etc..

Books

- ☐ Astrology
- ☐ Ayurveda
- ☐ Cookbook
- ☐ Fungshui
- ☐ Health
- ☐ Homeopathy
- ☐ Mythology
- ☐ Music
- ☐ Philosophy
- ☐ Religion
- ☐ Spirituality
- ☐ Tantra
- ☐ Yoga
- ☐ Vastu

For Export Enquiries :email us at
musicmandir@yahoo.com

FOR MALE CHILD
(66)

Those who want to get a male child should recite the following Mantra for 108 times until he gets a male child.

Aum Hreem Sreem Sidha Budha Maalaa Ambike Mama Sarvaa Sidhim Dehi Dehi Hreem Nama:

Direction	:	East
Day	:	Thursday
Recitation	:	11 Malas for 90 days. Offer one white flower to lord Krishna after every Mala.
Dress	:	Pure Silk white/cream
Mala	:	Pearl or Rudraksh
Asan	:	Mrigchala

TO CURE DOG BITE
(67)

For relief from dog bite, apply Bhasma (ash) recited with the following Mantra.

Sovana Kanjola'u Raajaa-dhushu Piyayi Gaha'u
Na Au-dhaayi Bhasmaantha Hoyi Jaayi.

Direction	:	North
Day	:	Tuesday
Recitation	:	108 times daily for 21 days
Dress	:	Yellow
Mala	:	Rudraksh
Asan	:	Mrigchala
Deity	:	Your own God/Goddess
Time	:	Before 10.00 a.m.

TO CURE FEVER
(68)

Take a saffron-coloured thread, recite the following Mantra for 21 times and make 7 knots in the thread. Tie the thread around the waist of the person suffering from fever. Fever will be cured.

Aum Chanda Kapaalinee Sheshaanu Jweram Bandha
Sayimla Jweram Bandha Velaa Jweram Bandha
Visham Jweram Bandha mahaa Jweram Bandha
Ta: Ta: Swaahaa.

Direction	:	North
Day	:	Any day
Recitation	:	7 Malas
Dress	:	Yellow
Mala	:	Tulsi
Asan	:	Cotton

TO ACQUIRE PROSPERITY
(69)

The Mantra consists of 31 Sanskrit alphabets. This Mantra contains the meanings of almost all that a man requires in his life. One will acquire all prosperity.

Aum Arham Nama: Aum Hreem Hreem Hreem. Aum Sreem Sreem Sreem. Aum Preem Preem. Aum Breem Breem Breem. Aum Bhreem Bhreem Bhree. Bhreem Bhreem Bhreem. Hum Phat Swaahaa.

Direction	:	West
Day	:	Thursday
Dress	:	Yellow
Asan	:	Yellow cotton
Deity	:	Durga
Time	:	Before 8.00 a.m. and in evening between 7.00 p.m. and 8.00 p.m.

FOR SIDDHI
(70)

The following Mantra is normally recited
on Monday by facing the Moon.
Recite for 1100 times on that day.
You will have complete Siddhi of Knowledge.
Thereafter you can be a master of all
Sadhna (Knowledge).

Aum Arhan-mukha Kamala Vaasini Paaopaathma
Kshayam
kari Srutha Jnaana Jwaalaa Sahasthra Jwelithe
Sarswathee
Mathpaapam Hana Hana Daha Daha Kshaam
kseheem
kshoom kshowm ksha: ksheera Dhavale Amritham
Sambhave
Vam Vam Ham Ham Swaahaa.

FOR MANTRA SIDDHI
(71)

One can have complete Mantra Siddhi of the following Mantra, if one recites it for 1100 times on Solar or Lunar Eclipse day. Recitation of this Mantra amidst or at the beginning of debate or any examination will give you sure success.

Aum Namo Bhagavathe Mahaa-Maaye Ajithe Aparaajithe

Thrylokta Maathe Vindhyese Sarve Bhootha Bhayaavaha

Maaye Maaye Ajithe Vashya Kaarike Bhramsa Bhraamini

Shoshini Dhroove Kaarine Lalathi Nethraa-shani Maarani

Pravaahani Rana haarini Jaye Vijaya Jam Bhani

Khageshwaree Khage Prokhe Hara Hara Praana Khinkhinee

Khinkhinee Vidhoona Vidhoona Vajra-hasthe Shoshaya

Shoshaya Thrisoola Hasthe Shata-vaagam Kapaala Dhaarini

Mahaa pishita marsa sini Maa-nu-shaardha Dharma
Praavrtha

Shareere Nara shira Maalaam Grandhitha Dhaarinee
Nisrubhini

hara Hara Praanaanu Marma Chedini Sahasthra
Shreersha

Sahasthra Vaahane Sahasra Nethre He Hva Hva
He Hva Hva

He He Sha Sha Ga Ga Ghu Ghu Cha Cha Jee Jee
Hreem Hreem

Thri Thri Kha Kha Hasanee Thrylokya Vinaashini
Phat Phat

Simhe Roope Kha: Gaja Roope Ga; Trylokhyo
Dare Samudra Mekhale Grnha Grnha Phat Phat
He HE Hum Hum Prum PRUM Hana Hana Maaya
Maaye Bhootha Prasave Parama Siddha Vidhye
Ha: Ha: Hum Hum Phut Phut Swaahaa.

Direction	:	East
Day	:	Wednesday
Recitation	:	1.25 Lac
Dress	:	White
Mala	:	Emrald or Green stone
Asan	:	Multi-colour cotton cloth
Deity	:	Lord Shiva
Time	:	Before 8.00 a.m.

FOR PERSONAL PROBLEMS
(72)

Recite the following Mantra during midnight in a complete naked posture. Then go to sleep. You will have the answer to all your problems in your dreams.

Aum Kiri Kiri Swaahaa.

Direction	:	North
Day	:	Tuesday
Recitation	:	Just count on fingers 108 times at night
Asan	:	Black sheet on your bed
Deity	:	Lord Shiva

TO CURE DANGEROUS DISEASES
(73)

Water recited with the following Mantra may be given to the person suffering from any disease. There will be complete relief from some diseases depending upon the intensity and some relief in dangerous diseases.

Aum Lam Vam Ram Yam Ksham Ham Sam Maathangini Swaahaa.

Direction	:	North
Day	:	Any day
Recitation	:	7 Malas
Mala	:	Tulsi
Asan	:	Cotton
Dress	:	Yellow

TO CURE FEVER
(74)

Hold the bunch of hair of the patient suffering from fever and recite the following Mantra for 21 times and tie 21 knots. Fever will vanish.

Aum Panchathmaaya Swaahaa.

Direction	:	North
Day	:	Any day
Recitation	:	7 Malas
Dress	:	Yellow
Mala	:	Tulsi
Asan	:	Cotton

TO STOP STAMMERING
(75)

Recite the following Mantra 2100 times. While reciting the Mantra the Sadhaka should pass his hands over the body of the patient having stammering problems. Give stress over the neck and navel.

Ga Cha Ha U Kupaa'u Uru Chinda'u Muhu-chinda'u

Pumchu Chinda'u Chindi Chindi Bhindi Bhindi Thruti

Thruti Jaahi Jaahi Jaahi Nisamnthaanu.

Direction	:	North
Day	:	Tuesday
Dress	:	Yellow
Mala	:	Rudraksh
Asan	:	Mrigchala
Deity	:	Your own God/Goddess

FOR FULFILLMENT OF
PERSONAL DESIRES
(76)

Recite the following Mantra for 1008 times during the month of Jyeshtha. Goddess Padmavati will be pleased and bestow on the Sadhaka the boon he wants.

Aum kleem Bleem Leem Ghreem Ghreem Sreem Kali Kunda Bhagavathee Swaahaa.

Direction	:	East
Day	:	Thursday
Recitation	:	108 times before 8.00 a.m.
Mala	:	Lotus
Asan	:	Multi-coloured cloth
Deity	:	Lord Shiva

TO SEE FAVOURITE DEITY
(77)

Recitation of the following Mantra for 2100 times for 41 days will enable the sadhaka to have Darshan (view) of a Hindu Goddess.

Aum Aam Kroom Hreem Nithye Kalam De Mada Drave Em Kleem Hrasowm Padmavathee Devee Thripuraji-thripura Kshobhinee Thrylokyam Kshobhaya
Kshobahya Shtree Vargam Aakarshaya Aakarshaya Bleem Hreem: Nama:

Direction	:	East
Day	:	Tuesday
Recitation	:	101 malas daily from 6.00 p.m. to 10.00 p.m.
Dress	:	White
Mala	:	Rudraksh or red pearl
Asan	:	White
Place	:	Bank of river or place of worship

TO ACHIEVE SARVA SIDDHI
(78)

The following Mantra will help the sadhaka to have Sarva Siddhi (mastery of all). Recite the Mantra 2100 times daily for 90 days.

Aum Hreem Sreem Padma Padmaasane Sree Dharenedra Priye Padmavathee Sriyam Mama Kuru Kuru Durithaani Hara Hara Sarva Dushtaanam Mukham Bandhaya Bandhaya Hreem Swaahaa.

Direction	:	East
Day	:	Thursday
Recitation	:	11 Malas for 41 days in morning and evening after taking bath.
Dress	:	Pure silk white
Mala	:	Rudraksh
Asan	:	Mrigchala
Deity	:	Lord Vishnu or your own Guru

TO INCREASE KNOWLEDGE
(79)

Drink the holy water by reciting the following Mantra for 108 times. You will have increased knowledge and intelligence. Repeat it for 21 days.

Aum Namo Bhagvathi Mahaa Vidhyaa Chakreswaree

Ehi Ehi Sheeghram Draam Bhroom Grhna Grhna Aum

Hreem Sahasthra Vadane Kumaari Shikhanda Vaahane

Srukle Srukle Gaathre Hreem Sathya Vaadini Nama:

Direction	:	East
Day	:	Wednesday
Recitation	:	2.25 lac
Dress	:	White
Mala	:	Green stone
Asan	:	White
Deity	:	Sarswati Ma
Time	:	8.00 a.m.

TO CURE FROM DISEASES
(80)

Take a small red thread of 1-1/4 meter length and recite the following Mantra for 21 times. Tie this thread on any part of the body of the person suffering from any disease. He will be cured.

Aum Namo Devaadhi Devaaya Nama: Simha Vyaaghra Raksha Vaahane Kati Chakra Krtha Mekhale chandraadhi Pathaye Bhagavathi Ghantaa-dhi-pathaya Tanam Tanam Shabdaadhi-pathaye Swaahaa.

Direction	:	North
Day	:	Any day
Recitation	:	7 Malas
Dress	:	Yellow
Mala	:	Tulsi
Asan	:	Cotton

FOR INFATUATION
(81)

Recite the following Mantra for 1100 times in a completely naked posture just before going to bed. All will be infatuated. Recite the name of the person in place of AMUK.

Aum Namo Bhagvathi Mahaa Mohinee Jambanee Sthambhanee Vashee Karanee Pura Kshobhinee Sarva shatru Vidraavanee Aum Aam Kron Hraam reem Prom Johi Johi Mohi Mohi Kshubha Kshubha Kshobhaya Amukm Vashee Kuru Kuru Swaahaa.

Direction	:	East
Day	:	Thursday
Recitation	:	108 times for 90 days
Dress	:	Yellow
Mala	:	Rudraksh
Asan	:	Mrigchala
Deity	:	Your own Guru
Time	:	Before 8.00 a.m.

TO BRING GOOD LUCK
(82)

The following Mantra daily will bring in good luck. Sadhaka will be liked by all and be capable to do wonders.

Aum Namo Bhagvathi Aparthi Chakre Jagathsam Mohinee Jgad unmaadinee Nayna Manoharee He He Aananda Paramaanade Parama Nirvaana Kaarinee
Kleem, Klyaana Devee Hreem Aprathi Chakre Phat
Vichakraaya Swahaa.

Direction	:	West
Day	:	Thursday
Recitation	:	7 Malas in a day before 8.00 a.m.
Mala	:	Rudraksh
Asan	:	Mrigchala
Deity	:	Your own Guru

VASHIKARAN
(83)

If the Sadhaka recites this Mantra before the female folk belonging to the kingly families, even they all will become his subordinates. For complete Siddhi of this Mantra take the flower of Lal kaner and recite 1 lakh times.

Aum namo Bhgvathi Aparthi Chakre Jagthsamohna kaari Siddhwe Sidhartha Kleem Klinne Madadrave Sarva Kaamaartha Saddhinee aam Em Oom Hithakaree
yasaskaree Prabham Karee Manoharee Vasham Karee
Sroom Ha Sa Bhroom Drrom Krum Draam Dreem Aprathi Chakre Phat Vichakraaya swaahaa.

Direction	:	East
Day	:	Friday
Recitation	:	108 times for 41 days
Dress	:	White
Mala	:	Chotti Elaichi
Asan	:	Cotton

TO OVERCOME BAD HABITS
(84)

Recite this Mantra, bad temperament and bad habits will vanish. In addition poison of any kind will not enter your body. It is suggested that the Sadhaka of this Mantra should recite it for 90 days atleast.

Savaayam Nnamo Bhagavatho Rshabhaaya Namhe Guru

Paadebhya Hadyu Hadu Kala Kala Simi Simi Grhvaa

Grhvaa Dhanum Dhanum Roombha Roombha Aavisha

Aavisha Maavilamva Maavilamva Sheegram Kuru Kuru

Suroo Suroo Muroo Muroo Vandha Vandha Daha Daha Chintha Chintha Shubha Shubha Veera Veera Bhanja Bhanja Mahaaveera Mahaaveera Grasa Grasa Marda

Marda He Hym He Dhum Dhum Me Me Me Budha Budha Hasa Hasa Hasa Keli Keli Mahaakeli Ta: Phat Phat Phuroo Phuroo Sarva grahaana Dhunu Mahaasaathwa

Vajrapaani Durdaa thaanam Damaka Chara Chara Chara kaka kaka kaka Yathaa Nushasthosthi Bhagavathaa Rshabha devena Thathaa Prathi pradhya edham Grham Graha Suvajra
Moordhaan Phaalaya Mahaa Vanthraadhipathji Sarva Bhoothaadhi Pathi Vajra Mervala Vajra Kaala Hum Hum Routhu Routhu Jayathi Vajra Paanir Mahaavala: Durdha Ra Ra Krodha Chanda Dhuroo Dhuroo Dhaave Dhaave Hee
Hvaa Hrowm Hvaa Ham Hvaa Kshaa Kshaa Ho Ho Kshow Kshow Hy Hy Kshum Kshum Ksham Ksham Ksham Ksha: So-dhar-maa-dhi-pathi Rshabha Swaami-raajna-payathi Swaahaa.

Direction	:	East
Day	:	Thursday
Recitation	:	108 times for 90 days
Dress	:	Yellow
Mala	:	Rudraksh
Asan	:	Mrigchala
Deity	:	Your own Guru
Time	:	Before 8.00 a.m.

FOR AUSPICIOUS EVENTS
(85)

Recite the following Mantra for 108 times. You will always have abundant profit in all the dealings and auspicious events will take place throughout your life.

Aum namo Bhavathyam Apa Kushmaandi Mahaavidhya
Kanaka Prabhe Simha Ratha Gaaminee Thrylokya
Kshobhanee Ehma Ehma Mama Chinthitham Kaarya
Kuru Kueru Bhaghvathee Swaahaa.

Direction	:	West
Day	:	Sunday
Recitation	:	3.25 Lac
Dress	:	Yellow
Mala	:	Rudraksh
Asan	:	Mrigchala
Deity	:	Lakshmi
Time	:	6.00 a.m. to 8.00 a.m.

KARAN PISHACHINI
(86)

You will have complete siddhi (master) of the Mantra. Thereafter you can use the Mantra on others. Method is that the Sadhaka should take bath and recite purificatory mantra first and then recite the following Mantra for 9 times in the right ear of the person who is in trouble. Solutions to the problem will appear in his dreams.

Aum Hreem Karne Pishaachinee Anodha Sathyavaadinee Mama Karna Avathra Avathra Sathyam Kathaya Kathaya Atheetha Anaagatha Varthamaanam Darshaya Darshaya Ehma Ehma Aum Hrim Karna Pishaachinee Swaahaa.

Direction	:	East
Day	:	Wednesday
Recitation	:	1.25 Lac
Dress	:	White
Mala	:	Emrald or green stone
Asan	:	Multi-colour cotton cloth
Deity	:	Lord Shiva
Time	:	Before 8.00 a.m.

FOR OVERALL SUCCESS
(87)

Recite the following Mantra in the morning for overall success.

Aum Namo Bhagvatho Parshwa Chandraaya Mahaaveery
Paraakramaaya Aparaajitha Shaasanaaya Samsaara
Pramardhanaaya Sarva shatru Vasham Karaay Kimnara
Kim Purusha Garuda Gandharva, Yaksh, Rakshasa, Bhootha
Jweram Vyaadhi Vinaashanyaa Kaala Dushta mantro
Chaadanaaya Sarva Dushta Graha Chedanaaya Sarva Rishu
Pranaasanaaya Aneka Mudraa Kotaa Kotee Shatha Laksha
Spothanaaya Vajra Srnkala Chedanaaya Vajra Mushti
Samchoorn naaya Chandra Haasa-chethanaaya Sudarsshana

Chakra Sphotanaaya Sarva Para
Chedanaaya Sarvaatma
Mantra Rakshanaaya Sarvaartha Kaama
Saathanaaya
Vishraan kushaaya Dhranedraaya Padmaavathi
Sahithaaya
Hili Hili Mili Mili Kili Kili Mshu Mahu Dili Dili
Paramaartha
Saadhinee Pacha Pacha Paya Paya Dhama Dhama
Dhara Dhara
Chinda Chinda Bhinda Bhinda Muncha Muncha
Paathaala
Vaasinee Padmaavathi Aajnaapayathi Hum Phat
Swaahaa.

Direction	:	West
Day	:	Thursday
Recitation	:	7 Malas in a day before 8.00 a.m.
Mala	:	Rudraksh
Asan	:	Mrigchala
Deity	:	Your own Guru

TO REMOVE EVIL EFFECT FROM CHILD
(88)

Recite the following Mantra by touching the body of the child. Drishti Dosha (evil effect) can be mitigated.

Aum Nameh Bhagavathe Paarshwatheertha Naathaaya Vajra Sphotnaaya, Vajra Maahavajra, Sarva Jweraqm, Aathma

Chakshu, para chakshu, pretha chakshu, Bhoota chakshu, Dakinee chakshu, Shaakinee chakshu, Simhaaree Chakshu,

Maatha Chakshu, Pitha Chakshu, Vattaaree, Chamaaree, Etheshaam, Sarveshaam Drshti Bandhaya Bandhaya Aavalathe

Sree Paarshwanaathaaya Nama:

Direction	:	East
Day	:	Monday
Recitation	:	11 Malas daily for 41 days
Mala	:	Rudraksh
Asan	:	Black cotton

FOR SARVA SIDDHI
(89)

Daily recitation of the following Mantra will give the Sadhaka Sarva Siddhi. All kinds of diseases will be cured.

Aha Ghonasavijjaaye Manthyhim Javathi Sathavaaraa'u

Pachaapi Vanthi Thoyam Patanthi Aha Ghonasa Vijja

Vijja Manthoyam Aum Nameh Shri Ghona Sa Hare Hare

Vare Vare Thare Thare Va: Va: Vala Vala laam Laam Raam

Raam Reem Reem Room Room Rowm Rowm Rasa Rasa

Kshoom Kshom Hreem Hreem Hrom Haam Bhagvathee Sree

Ghona Se Gha: Gha: Gha: Gha: Gha: Sa: Sa: Sa: Sa: Sa: Ha: Ha:

Ha: Ha: Ha:, Va: Va: Va: Va: Va:, Da: Da: Da: Da: Da:, Tta: Tta:

Tta: Tta: Tta:, Ga: Ga: Ga: Ga: Ga; Vara
Vihamgama Nuje
Kshmaam Ksheem Kshmoom Kshmowm Kshma:
Kshmaam
Ree Shoshay a Shoshaya Ta: Ta: Ta: Sree Ghona
Se Swaahaa.

Direction	:	West
Day	:	Thursday
Dress	:	Yellow
Asan	:	Yellow cotton
Deity	:	Durga
Time	:	Before 8.00 a.m. and in evenin between 7.00 and 8.00 p.m.

FOR PROFITS
(90)

Recitation of the following Mantra daily will give you ample profit in your transaction.

Aum Nameh Indra Bhooda Ganaharassa Savva Labdhi
Karassa Mama Srudhim Vrdhim Kuru Kuru Swaahaa.

Direction	:	West
Day	:	Thursday
Dress	:	Yellow
Asan	:	Yellow cotton
Deity	:	Durga
Time	:	Before 8.00 a.m. and in evening between 7.00 and 8.00 p.m.

TO CONTROL TROUBLE
(91)

Recitation of the following Mantra daily 21 times, will enable you to be free from troubles caused by your enemy and your wishes will be fulfilled.

Aum Hreem Krshna Vaasase Shatha Vadane Shata Sahasthra
Simha Koti Vaahane Para Vidyaa Udhyaadane Sarva Dushta
Nikandane Sarva Dushta Bhakshane Aparaajitha Prathyangire
Mahaavale Shatru Kshaye Swaahaa.

Direction	:	East
Day	:	Friday
Recitation	:	21 Malas
Dress	:	Yellow
Mala	:	Rudraksh
Asan	:	Cotton

FOR PROFITS
(92)

Recitation of the following Mantra daily will give you ample profit in your transaction.

Aum namo Indra Bhooda Ganahassa avva Labdhi Karasaa
Mama Srudhim Vrdhim Kuru Kuru swaahaa.

Direction	:	East
Day	:	Monday
Recitation	:	108 times for 41 days
Dress	:	White
Mala	:	Pearl
Asan	:	Cotton cloth of seven colours
Deity	:	Lord Shiva
Time	:	9.00 a.m. to 10.00 a.m.

TO DESTROY ENEMY
(93)

Take cloth used on the dead body from the burial ground. Write the following Mantra with poison and human blood mixed. At the end of the Mantra, write the name of your enemy. Bury the cloth in CHORASTA. Your enemy will slowly be hunted by the super natural evil forces and will suffer in all respect. Nobody on earth can save him. The only remedy is to dig out the cloth buried. The moment the cloth so buried is taken out the person will return to the normal state.

Aum Hrim Lrim Kshim Bhrim Srim He He Hara Hara Amukum Mahaa-bhoothena Grnhaapaya Grnhaa-paya Laya Laya sheeghram Sheeghram Bhaksha Bhaksha Khaahi Khaahi Hum Phatow.

Direction	:	South
Day	:	Any day
Recitation	:	1.25 Lac
Dress	:	Black
Mala	:	Baheda
Asan	:	Lion's skin
Deity	:	Before Kali Ma

TO MITIGATE EVILS
(94)

Water recited for 21 times for 21 days with the following Mantra if given to drink, all kind of evils can be mitigated.

Arahanthaanam Jinaanam Bhagavanthaanam Mahaapa
Bhaavaanam Ho'u Namo U Maayee Saahim Tho Savva
Dukha Haro, Johi Jinaanapabhaavo Para Mittee-naancha
Janja Maahapaam Sanghaamijonu Bhaavo Avayara Ujalam Misoyitha.

Direction	:	South
Day	:	Saturday
Recitation	:	108 times for 41 days
Dress	:	Black
Mala	:	Beheda
Asan	:	Black
Deity	:	Bhairon

TO CONTROL TROUBLES
(95)

Recitation of the following Mantra daily in morning will protect you from all possible troubles.

Muhi Chandappaha Jjhahiyayi Jinuma Thayi Paarasa Vathu

Eenaa Emu Cha Em Muuchakiya Ko Hee Lanaha Samuthu.

Aum Shaanthe Shaanthi Prade Jaga Jeeva Hitha Shanthi Kare

Aum Hrim Bhayam Prsama Prasma Bhagavthi Shaanthe-

mamashanthi Kuru Kuru Shivam Kuru Kuru Nirroopadravam

Kuru Kuru Aum Hraam Hrim Hrom Hra: Shanthe Swaahaa.

Aum Nameh'u Raho Veera Mahaaveere Senaveere Vardhamaana Veere Jayanthe Aparaajiye Bhagavau Arahassa

jinintha Varveera Aayanasaa Ku Samaya
Mayappanaa Sanassa
Bhagava'u Samana Sangharsam Mem Sidha-
asidhaayiyaa
saasana Devini Vigham Kuna'u saanishpam
Swaahaa.

Direction	:	North
Day	:	Tuesday
Recitation	:	Just count on fingers 108 times at night
Asan	:	Black sheet on your bed
Deity	:	Lord Shiva

FOR PROTECTION FROM TROUBLE
(96)

Recitation of the following Mantra for 21000 times when you are in extreme trouble will completely protect you and produce favourable results.

Aum Hraam Hrim Kram Krim Kram Kra:
Sreeshesh
raajaaya Nmeh Hoom Ha: HA: Vam Kre Kre SA:
SA:
Swaaha:

Direction : North

Day : Tuesday

Recitation : 21000 times

Asan : Black sheet on your bed

Deity : Lord Shiva

FOR INFATUATION
(97)

Take water in both hands and recite the following Mantra. Thereafter drink the water by uttering the name of the person you want to infatuate. He/She will be infatuated towards you.

Aum Namo Rathnathrayasya Aavatuka Daarukavi Daaruka
Vivatuka Vivatu Vivatu Daaruka Swaahaa Swaahaa Swaahaa
Swaahaa Swaahaa Swaahaa Swaahaa Swaahaa Swaahaa
Swaahaa Swaahaa Swaahaa. Kato Phe Mam Nameh Kshipragaamini Kuru Kuru Vimale-Swaahaa.

Direction	:	East
Day	:	Thursday
Dress	:	Yellow
Mala	:	Rudraksh
Asan	:	Mrigchala
Deity	:	Your own Guru
Time	:	Before 8.00 a.m.

TO INCREASE KNOWLEDGE
(98)

Recite the following Mantra
for 108 times, thrice a day
for seven days.
Your knowledge will increase.

Aum Arapachana Dhim Swaahaa.

Direction	:	West
Day	:	Thursday
Mala	:	Rudraksh
Asan	:	Mrigchala

FOR RELIEF FROM PAIN
(99)

Recite the following Mantra for 108 times. You will get relief from pain.

Paarshw-parva'u Trishooladhaaree Srula Bhanjayi
Srula Phodayi Thaasulaya Jaya.

Direction : North

Day : Any day

Recitation : 7 Malas

Dress : Yellow

Mala : Tulsi

Asan : Cotton

NAVGREH MANTRAS

MANTRA FOR SUN

Recite the following Mantra for one lac times within 41 days.

> *Aum Nsamoh-arha-the Bhagavathe Padhya-Prabha-theer-than-Karaaya Kusulayaksha Manovegaa Yakshee Sahithaaya*
>
> *Aum Aam Krom Hrim Hran: Aadithya-mahaagraha (Mama Kutumba-vargasya) Sarva dushta-graha Raga Kastha-vivarane*
>
> *Kuru Kuru Sarva-Shanti Kuru Kuru Sarva Samridhi Kuru Kuru*
>
> *Eshta sampada Kuru Kuru Anishta Nishasanam Kuru Kuru kaama-managalyoth-savam Kuru Kuru Hoom Phat.*

Or

Recite the following Mantra for 1.25 lac times within 21 days. Do surya namaskar everyday early in the morning. Idol of sun be consecrated at the pooja place and pooja performed with red flowers and red sandalwood powder or paste.

AUM Hran Hrin Hron Sai Suraye Nameh:

Or

Recite the following Mantra daily 21 times in the morning.

Aum Divaakaraaya Vidmahe.
Prabhaakaraaya Dheemahi.
Thanno Aadithya Prajodayath.

Or

Recite the following Mantra 21 times daily in the morning.

Aum Bhaaskaraaya Vidmahe.
Divaakraaya Dheemahi.
Tanno Surya Prachodayat.

Or

Recite the following Mantra daily 21 times. All the evil effect caused by the Sun will be removed.

Aum Hran Hrin Sa; Aum Bhoorbhuva: Swaha:
Aum Aakrshnena Rajasaa Varthamaano Nivesha-
Yanta-mrtham Mrityar-jna. Hiranyena Savithaa
Rathena Devee Yaathi Bhuvanaaji Pasyanu.
Aum SA: Swa: Bhuva: Bhoo: Aum SA: Hron Hran
Aum Sooryaye Nameh:

MANTRA FOR MOON

Recite the following Mantra for 21000 times within 11 days.

Aum Namo arhathe Bhagavathe Sreemathe
Chandraprabha-theerthan-karaaya Vijaya
Yaksha Jwaala Maalinnee Yakshee Sahithaaya
Aum Aam Krim Hrim Hran: Somamahaa-grahaa
Mama Dushta-graha Rogakasta Nivaaranam
Sarva Shanthi Cha Kuru Kuru Hoom Phat.

Or

Recite the following Mantra 11 times daily in morning or evening.

Dadhi-Sankha-Tusaabham Sto-darnava-Sambhavam-Namaami Saasinaam Somam Samboorna Mukuta Bhushanam

Or

Recite the following Mantra for 21000 times within 11 days. Thereafter give salute (Namaskar) to the Moon in the evening. If possible white dress may be used.

Aum Sraam Sreem Srown Sa: Chandramase Nama:

MANTRA FOR MARS

Recite the following Mantra for 11000 times within 21 days.

AUM Namon-arhathe Bhagavathe Vaasu-Poojya-theer-thankaraaya Shanmukha-yaksha Gaandhaaree Yakshee Sahithaayya Om Aam Krom Hreem Hra: Mangala kuja Mahaa-graha Mama Dushta-graha Rogakashta Nivaaranam Sarva shanthi cha kuru kuru Hoom Phat.

Or

Recite the following mantra for 10000 times within 21 days. Pooja may be performed with red sandalwood powder or paste and red-coloured flowers.

AUM Karaam Kreem Krowm Sa: Bhowmaaya Namah:

Or

Recite the following Mantra daily 21 times.

Dharanee Garbha Sambhutam Vidyut Kaanti
Samaprabhaa kumaaram Sakthee Hastam Cha
Mangalam Praanamaami Aham.

Or

Recite the following Mantra 21 times daily.

Aum Namo Mangalaaya Nama: Sarva
Dosham Naasham Karethu Swaahaa.

MANTRA FOR MERCURY

Recite the following Mantra for 32000 times within 41
days.

Aum Namo arhath Bhagavathe Sreemathe
Malleetheerthan-karaaya Kubera-yaksham
Aparaajitha Yakshee Sahithaaya Aum Aam
Krom Hreem Hra: Budha-Mahaa-graha
Mama Dushta-graha Roga Kashta Nivaaranam
Sarva Shhanthi ChA Kuru Kuru Hoom Phat.

Or

Recite the following Mantra for 11000 times within 11
days.

Aum Braam Breem Browm SA: Budhaaya Namah.

Or

Recite the following Mantra for 14000 times within 21 days.

> *Priyanga Gukali-ka-shyaamam*
> *Roopeena-Prathimam Budham.*
> *Soumyam Soumya-guno-petham*
> *Tam Budham Pranamaamya-ham.*

Or

Recite the following Mantra 21 times daily.

> *AUM Bram Brim Browm Sa: Bhur Bhuva Swaha:*
> *AUM Ud-budha-yaswaagne Prathijaagr-hithwa-*
> *mishtaapootha Saha Sujethaa-mayanvha.*
> *Asmimntha-sandhasthe-ardha-yukthaarisman*
> *viswadeva Yajamaanascha Seedathe. Aum Swah:*
> *Bhuva: Bhu: Aum Browm Breem Braam Aum*
> *Budhaaya Namah:*

MANTRA FOR JUPITER

Recite the following Mantra 21000 times within 21 days.

> *Aum Namon-arhathe Bhagavathe Srmathe Vardhamaana*
> *Therthan-karaaya Maathanga-yaksha Sidhaayine-yakshe*
> *Sahitthaaya Aum Krom Hreem Hra: Guru-Mahaa-graha*
> *Mama Dushtaa-graha Rog-kahta Nivaaranam Sarva*
> *Shaanthi*
> *Cha Kuru Kuru Hoom Phat.*

Or

Recite the following Mantra for 19000 times within 21 days.

Aum Jhraam Jhreem Jhrown Sa: Guruave Namah

Or

Recite the following Mantra for 21000 times within 11 days.

Dvaanancha Rshee-naancha Gurum
Kaanchana-Snnibham. Budhi-bhootham
Trilokesham Tham Namaami Brhaspathim.

MANTRA FOR VENUS

Recite the following Mantra for 16000 times within 21 days.

Aum Namon arhathe Bhagavathe Sreemathee
Pushpadanta Theerthan-karaaya Maaqthanga-yaksha
Sidhaayinee-yakshee Sahithaaya Aum Krom Hrim Hran
Guru-Mahaa-graha Mama Dushtaa-graha Rog-Kashta
Nivaaranam Sarva Shaanthi Cha Kuru Kuru Hoom Phat.

Or

Recite the following Mantra for 16000 times within 21 days. Pooja be performed with white flowers and white sandalwood paste or powder.

AUM Draam Drem Drown SA: Shukraya Namah:

Or

Recite the following Mantra for 21 times daily.

Himauna-mrnaalaabham Daithyaanam Paramam
Gurum. Sarva-shaastra-pravaktaaram Bhaargavam
ranaa-maamyaham.

If Venus is severely afflicted, observe fast on Friday and distribute sweets and rice among the poor.

MANTRA FOR SATURN

Recite the following Mantra for 26000 times within 26 days.

> *Aum Namon-arahgte Bhagavathe Sreemathe*
> *Muni Suvratha Theerthan-karaaya Varuna-yaksha*
> *Bahu-roopinee-yakshi Sahithaaya Aum Aam Krom*
> *Hreem Hra: Shani-mahaa-graha Mama Dushta-graha*
> *Raga-kashta Nivaaranaa Sarva Shaanthi Cha Kuru*
> *Kuru Hoom Phat.*

Or

Recite the following Mantra for 26000 times within 26 days.

> *Aum Praam preem prown Sa: Shaanaye Nameh:*

Or

> *Aum Khaam Kheem Khown SA: Shanaye Namah.*

Or

Recite the following Mantra 11 times daily.

> *Aum Neelaanchana-samaa-bhaasam Ravi-*
> *puthram Yamaa-grajam Chaayaa-marthaanda*
> *-sambhootham Tama Nsamamim Shanaischaram.*

If Saturn is severely afflicted, distribute oil and blankets among the poor.

MANTRA FOR RAHU

Recite the following Mantra for 18000 times within 21 days.

Aum Namon-arhathe Bhagavathe Sreemathe
Nemi-theerthan-karaaya Sarvaasht-yaksha
Kushmaandi-yakshee Sahithaaya Aum aam
Krom Hreem Hra: Raahu-mahaagraha Mama
Dushta-raha Roga-kashta Nivaarana Sarva
Shaanthi Cha Kuru Kuru Hoom Phat.

Or

Recite the following Mantra for 18000 times within 21 days.

AUM Bhraam Bhreem Bhrown SA: Raahuve Namah:

MANTRA FOR KETU

Recite the following Mantra for 7000 times within 11 days.

Aum Namon-arhathe Bhagavathe Sreemathe
paarshwa Theerthan-karaaya Dharaneedra-yaksha
Padmaavathee-yakshee Sahithaaya Aum Aam Krom
Hrim Hran Kethu mahaa-graha Mama Dushta-graha
Rogakshta Nivaanam Sarva Shanthi Cha Kuru Kuru Phat.

Or

Recite the following Mantra for 7000 times within 11 days.

Aum Praam Preem Prowm Sa: Kethuve namah:

NINE MANTRAS FOR INFATUATION

1. Aum Namo Krshna Savaraaya
   Valgu Valgu Ne Swaahaa.

2. Aum Namo Bhagavathee Gange
   Kaalee Kalee Mahaakaalee Swaahaa.

3. Aum Namo Bhgavathi Ppadmaavathee Vrshabha
   Vaahinee Sarva-jana Kshobhini Mama Chinthitha
   Karma Karma Kaarinee Aum Aum Hraam Hreem
   Hra:

4. Aum Namo Bhagvathee Rudraaya Aum Chamunde
   Amukasya Hrdyam Pivaami Chaamundinee Swaahaa.

Take water, recite the Mantra 1100 times and drink the water by thinking the name of the person you want to infatuate. He/She will be infatuated.

5. Aum Namo Bhagavathee Vasham Kari Swaahaa.

6. Aum Sugandavathee Sugandha Vadanaa
   Kaaminee Kaamesh-waraaya Swahaa Amuka
   Shtree Vasha Maanaya Maanaya.

7. Aum Deve Chanda Nirayi Karayio Haru
   Mandayi Raahadi Theenayi Thribhuvana
   Vasi Kiyaa Hreem Kiyayi Nilaadi.

Sandalwood paste (Chandan) recited with the following Mantra may be applied as tilak. All will be infatuated.

8. Aum Kaama Devaaya Kaama Vasham Karaaya
   Amukasya Hrdayam Sthambhaya Mohaya
   Vashamaanaya Swaahaa.

Take Sindoor, chandan paste and kumkum in equal proportion and recite the following Mantra seven times and use as tilaka. All will be infatuated. You may also take any eatable and give that after reciting the mantra to the person you want to infatuate.

9. Aum Devee Rudra Keshee Mantra Sesee Devee
   Jwaalaa Mukhi Soothi Jaaga Visi-vayittee
   Leyaavisee Haath Jotanthi Paaya Laaganthi
   Tam Talee Vaayanthi Saankala Modanthi Le
   Aa'u Kaanghada Naarasimha Veera Prachanda.

SIGNIFICANCE OF MANTRA ON FOURTH AND ELEVENTH LUNAR DAYS

All our festivals are based on astrological or astronomical principles but we have forgotten the significance of these for the purpose of Mantra. It is for the good of mankind that these festivals have been instituted. Due to passage of time and having forgotten the significance, we are sceptical about them, and we do not attach the necessary importance to them.

For mantra it is my object to prove my claim in the light of vishtikarana.

DEFINITION

A karana is half of tithi and tithi is the time taken by the moon to travel approximately 12 degrees of space with reference to the Sun, i.e. in astronomical language, the time taken for an increase of 12 degrees in the elongation of the Moon from the Sun. As the motion of the Moon is highly irregular, the duration of a tithi is never constant.

Since a karana is half of a tithi, its duration is the time taken by the Moon for an increase of 6 degrees in the elongation of the Moon from the Sun.

There are eleven Karanas of which 7 are moveable or Chara karanas and the remaining 4 are fixed or sthira karanas. Bava, Balava, Kaulava, Thaithula, Garaji, Vanija and Vishti or Bhadra are the chara Karanas whereas Sakuni, Chathushpadam, Nagam and kismsthugnam are the Sthira Karanas.

Sakuni begins with the second half of the fourteenth day of the dark fortnight (Krishna chaturdashi), then Chathushpadam, Nagam and Kimsthugnam come in order ending with the first half of the first day of the bright fortnight (Shukla padhyami). The movable Karanas rotate among the other tithis or lunar days, beginning with the second half of Shukla padyami. Garga state as follows:

Analysing the whole scheme, Vishti or Bhadra falls on the following days:

Shukla Paksha (bright fortnight): Chaturathi (fourth day) second half, Ashtamai (eight day) first half, Ekadasi (eleventh day) second half, Poornami (full Moon) first half.

Krishna paksha (Darka fortnight), Thritiya (third day) second half,

Sapthami (seventh day) first half, Dasami (tenth day) second half, chaturdashi (fourteenth day) first half.

FUNCTIONS ON VISHTI KARANA

· Vasishta says:

The functions to be celebrated on Vishtikaranas according to Vasishta are as follows: "Killing, binding, use of poisons, fire, arrows or instruments, cutting and use of black magic and uchattan Mantra etc. Functions using horses, buffaloes and camels will be successful on Vishitikarana day. One who wants to be prosperous in the world should not have an auspicious function on a vishtikarna. But if such a function be celebrated by one out of ignorance, everything will end in destruction." I think that no attention is paid to the evil effects of Vishtikarana in fixing Muhurathas for marriages, etc. Even in natal astrology, reference is made to the evil effects of Vishtikarana.

Jataka Parijata says:

"One born on Vishti will be an enemy of all, will commit evil deeds, of bad fame, independent and honoured by followers."

EXCEPTION

All Vishtikaranas are not considered as bad and there are exceptions to the general rule, Lalla says:

"Vishtikaranas coinciding with the second half of a tithi are benefic in daytime and those coinciding with the first half are good at night", says Kamalasana.

Brahma Siddhanta

This statement supports the earlier statement as regards the rule of exception.

MYTHOLOGICAL ORIGIN

Vishtikarana has a mythological origin. Sripathi says as follows: "When the Devas were defeated badly by the Daityas in a battle, Lord Shiva got angry and created out of his body Vishti with the face of a donkey, a long tail and three feet. She had seven hands, throat of a lion and narrow stomach. She destroyed the Daityas and so the Devas elevated her permanently to the position of karana".

A rational explanation of this is that when the Devas got defeated in a battle with the Daityas, Lord Shiva must have fixed Vishtikarana as a suitable time astrologically to ensure success for devas. Vishti is good for waging wars successfully as indicated in an earlier paragraph.

VIANAYAKA CHAUTHI

This is a great national festival for all of us and it has great astrological significance. Let us first give a short account of the origin of the function. The following account is taken from Skanda Purana.

Prince Satrajit performed penance to propitiate the Sun God who gave him the Syamanthak Mani, a gem of great brilliance. This previous stone yielded everyday 12 bharas of gold (one bhara is equal to 20 maunds i.e. 8 quintals). Satrajit looked brilliant like sun when he wore it. He had declined to part with it when Lord Krishna had expressed a desire to have it. Prasenjit, brother of Satrajit, once went for hunting wearing the Mani. He was killed by a lion who was later killed by Jambuvan. Jambuvan took the Mani to his cave. When Pransenjit did not return, a rumour spread that Lord Krishna had killed him to acquire the Mani. Lord Krishna disturbed by the rumour and to make his position clear, made a vigorous search for the missing Prince. He found the body of Prasenjit in the forest. Following the trail he reached the spot where the body of the lion was lying and thereafter the cave of Jambuvan enveloped in the brilliance of the Syamanthaka Mani. A duel was fought between the two for 20 days. Ultimately Lord Krishna won. The defeated Jambuvan gave the Mani to Lord Krishna and also his daughter Jambvati in marriage to Him.

When Lord Krishna returned with the mani the people of Dwarka were satisfied with His innocence. Satrajit also tendered apologies to Him.

However, Lord Krishna wanted to know the cause of the calumny and consulted Narada who told him that it was the result of His having seen the Moon on the fourth day of the dark fortnight. The Moon, he said, was under a curse from Lord Ganesha, who was once wandering in Devloka and the Moon, shining in full splendour, had laughed at his bloated belly and peculiar form. Lord Ganesha had got angry and had cursed him that those who would look at the Moon on the fourth lunar day of the lunar month would be subject to calumny. The only way to get over the trouble would be to propitiate Lord Ganesha. Lord Krishna had seen the Moon on the fourth day of the Lunar month and so became the victim of the false rumour.

Bhadarapada Shukla Chaturathi is the most significant day for propitiating Lord Ganesha to get over all obstacles. All the troubles can be removed by enchanting Mantra.

RATIONAL EXPLANATION

Lord Ganesha represents obstacles, troubles etc. These are caused by the malefic directions of the planets and even Lord Krishna was not exempt from the malefic operations of the planets and the only way by which we can get over the difficulties is through prayers and propitiation to the planets as ordained by the sages. Ordinary mortals must be doubly careful when they are under the malefic influence of the planets. The fourth Lunar day of the bright fortnight is the worst day astrologically exercising the baneful influences of a moon who is weak and malefic.

Let us consider the position of the Moon relative to the Sun, that is, its elongation in the several Vishtikaranas.

Vishtikarana Table

LUNAR DAYS (Shukla Paksha)

Chaturathi (4th day) 2nd half	42°-48°
Ashtami (8th day) 1st half	84°-90°
Ekadshi (11th day) 2nd half	126°-132°
Pournima (Full Moon) 1st half	168°-174°

LUNAR DAYS (Krishna Paksha)

Thritiya (3rd day) 2nd half	210°-216°
Saptami (7th day) 1st half	252°-258°
Dasami (10th day) 2nd half	294°-300°
Chaturdashi (14th day) 1st half	336°-342°

On the first two vishtikarana days, Moon's elongation is such that 45 degree and 90 degree aspects are included. They are the semi-square and square aspects of western astrology which are considered highly malefic. The first vishtikarana falls on the fourth lunar day which is the most malefic day according to our convention as the Moon is very week and therefore greater importance is attached to Chavithi. Lord Ganesha is propitiated on that day with great enthusiasm and religious fervour. The celebration of Vinayaka Chauithi is really the propitiation to mitigate the evil effects of Vishtikarana, i.e., the semi-square aspect between sun and Moon. Ashtmi—the lunar day, when the Moon's elongation from the Sun is 90 degree (Square aspect between Sun and Moon) is a day set apart for prayers, oblation to the Manes (Pitris), etc., but the practice appears to have fallen into disuse.

Significance of Ekadsi

Ekadsi or the eleventh lunar day, otherwise known as Hari Vasara, is a day of Mantra and prayer for all Hindus. It is a day of Vishtikarana, a day of malefic influence. Our wise sages had set apart that day for prayer, fasting and Mantra. Chauithi is dedicated to Lord Ganesha and Ekadshi to Lord Vishnu.

There is a practice amongst Hindus to fast on Shukla Ekadshi and not on the other Ekadshi of the Krishna Paksha or dark fortnight. The reason is now obvious.

Vishtikarana coincides with the second half of Dasami of Krishna Paksha; some orthodox persons begin fasting and reciting Mantras on the night of Dashmi and break their fast on Dwadasi in the early morning.

Eventually Dasami and Ekadshi of both the Pakshas have come to be considered as significant for Mantras.

OTHER DAYS

Tritiya (third day) of the dark fortnight is another day of Vishtikarana. It is a day when the elongation is 210 degree or subject to Shashtashtaka aspect. Pournima is a highly significant day and many religious teachers like Lord Buddha were born on a full Moon day of Vishtikrana. They renounced worldly prosperity and attained great spiritual eminence. It is a day of Sun opposition Moon when worldly prosperity is denied.

Varah Mihira in his Brihat Jataka states that the Moon in an angular (Kendra) position to the Sun is never conducive to worldly prosperity.

In the preceding paragraphs, the influence of Vishtikarana is explained. It is a day to be avoided for all functions associated with worldly prosperity but it is eminently suitable for spiritual practices. It is better to avoid a Vishtikarana as it is a day of malefic influence both according to western and Hindu methods. The approaches may be different, but the conclusions are always the same, whatever system of astrology we follow.

So let none scoff at the religious functions associated with Chaturathi and Ekadshi. One who fasts on Ekadshi is considered to attain Moksha. Such a person will be free from the malefic planetary influences and so will be happy. He will have peace of mind to think of God and attain Moksha.

Vishtikarana coincides with the second half of Ekadasi Tithi and this astronomical fact gives the clue to the rule that Ekadshi Tithi should not have Dashmi Vedha for celebration. If Dashmi tithi is less then 6 Ghatis (2 hours 24 minutes) or less than 4 ghatis (1 hour 36 minutes) according to another school before sunrise on the day of Ekadashi Tithi, the day is said to have Dashmi Vedha or afflicted by Dasami and Ekadashi is to be celebrated on the next day. This rule is quite obvious as fasting is to be done when Vishtikarana is in duration; breaking of fast should not coincide with the period when Vishtikarana is in duration. If this rule is not laid down by our sages, and Ekadshi is observed on a day when it begins, say an hour before sunrise on the next day of Dwadasi, when in the early morning fasting is to end. This should not happen according to our sages.

Our sages had laid down rules and regulations for the prosperity and happiness of the human race but, the modern educated persons look at them with scorn and attribute these rituals to ignorance and lack of scientific education.

KALA GYANA MANTRA

It is important to complete counting the beeds of the Mala 21 times while reciting the Mantra. The prayer rug, could be of cotton or wool and the Sadhana could be started on any night of the full moon. Once this sadhana is completed, no other ritual is required. Only incense is to be burnt. After the month of Anushthana one can require the power to know about anyone's past, present and future by just looking at him or her. One comes to know all the secrets about the person concerned and can see his future vividly. All his forecasts turn out to be correct.

This is a secret Mantra which is not to be imparted to anyone easily, unless he acquires prior permission from the siddh guru of the Siddhashrama.

The Mantra is given below.

Aum namo Bhagwate Brahmananda pada: Golkadi asankhya Brahmanda bhuvana nathaya shashanka shashanka goksheira karpura dhaval gatrava neelambodhi jalada patala- dhivyaktaswarupaya vyodhikarma, nirmulochhedana karaya jati jarayamarana, viashanaya, sansarakantaronmula naya achintya bala parakramaya ati pratimah chakraya trailokyadhishwaraya, shabdai ke trailokyadhin arivala bhuvana karkaya, sarvasatya hitaya, nij bhaktaya, abhishta phal pradaya bhaktyadhinaya Sura Surendradi mukutakoti dhrishtavada pithaya, ananta yuga nathaya, devadhidevaya dharmachakradhishwaraya, sarva vidya parameshwaraya, kuvidya vighna pradaya, tatpadapankaja shrayani yavani den sasana devate tribhuvana Sankshobhani,

Trilokya Shivapaharkarinini Shri adbhuta jataveda Shri Mahalakshmi Devi (amukasya sthavara jangama kritrim vishamukha sanharinim Sarvabhichara Karmapahrinim parvidyachhedani paramantra pranashinim ashta mahanaga kulichhatinim kaladonshra mrita kolyapinim (amukasya) sarvaroga pramochinim, Brahmavishu Rudendra Chandradityadigraha nakshotrapata marana bhaya pida mardin trailokya vishwaloka vanshakari bhuviloka hitakam Mahabhairavi Bhairva shastropadharini raudre, raudrarupdhari prasiddhe, siddha Vidyadhara yaksha jwalapata karala digantarale Mahavrishabha vahini, khetaka kripana trishula shakti chakrapasha sharasana Shiva virajamana Shodashardha bhuje ehi ehi lam jwala malinim hrim hrim hram hram hrim hraum hrah devan akarshaya akarshaya naga grahana akarshaya yaksha grahana akarshaya akarshayah gandharva grahan akarshaya bhut grahan akarshaya akarshaya divyatara grahan akarshaya akarshaya chaturashi jainya marga grahan akarshaya akarshaya akarshaya akhila mundit grahan akarshaya jangam grahan akarshaya akarshaya durgeshadi vidyagrahan akarshaya akarshaya Sarva naga vigraha vasi grahan akarshaya akarshaya Sarva naga nigraha vasi grahan akarshaya akarshay Sarva jalashaya vigraha vasi grahan akarshaya akarshaya Sarvasthala vasi grahan akarshaya akarhsya sarvat sthit grahan akarshaya akarshaya sarva shamshanvasi grahan akarshaya akarshaya sarva pavani vasi grahan akarshaya akarshava Sarv dharma shapadi shapa grahan akarshaya akarshaya Sarva giriguha durga vasi grahan akarshaya akarshaya akarshaya sara nathapanthi grahan akarshaya akarshaya sarvabhuvasi pret grahan akarshaya akarshaya akarshaya akarshaya vakra pinda grahan akarshaya akarshaya kata kata kampaya kampaya shirsha chalaya shirsha chalaya gatram chalaya gataram chalaya bahum chalaya bahum chalaya padam chalaya padam chalaya kar pallavan chalaya kar pallavan chalaya sarvanga halaya sarvanga chalaya lolaya lolaya dhun dhun kampaya kampaya shighra bhava taraya taraya grahi grahi grahya grahya akshaya akshaya aveshaya aveshya jwalum jwalamalinim hram khim vlum dram dram jwala jwala ra ra

*ra ra ra ra prajvala prjvala dhag dhag dhumaksha karanim
jwala vishoshaya vishoshaya devagrahan daha daha naga grahan
daha daha yaksha grahan daha daha yaksha grahan daha daha
gandharva grahan daha daha Brahma grahan daha daha raksha
grahan daha daha bhuta grahan daha daha divyantara grahan
daha daha chatasaashi janya marga grahan daha daha chaturvish
jin grahan daha daha sarva jatil grahan daha daha akhila
mundit grahan daha daha jangam grahan daha daha sarva
durgeshadi vidya grahan daha daha sarva nagingrahavasi grahan
daha daha sarva sthalvasi grahan, daha daha sarvantantariksha
vasi grahan daha daha shamshanavasi grahan daha daha sarva
pavanaharta grahan daha daha sarva dharma shapadi
goshapavasi grahan daha daha sarvagiriguha durgavasi grahan
daha daha shapita grahan dah daha sarvantha panthi grahan
daha daha sarvadhuvasi preta grahan daha daha (amuk grihe)
asadgati grahan daha daha vakrapinda grahan daha daha
sarvadushta grahan daha daha shatakoti yojane doshdayi grahan
daha daha sahokoti dosh daha daha asamudrat prithvi madye
devabhutapischachadi (amukasya) parikrit doshan tasya doshan
daha daha shatrukritabhichar doshan daha daha dhe dhe
sphotaya sphotaya maraya masraya dhhagi dhaagi dhagaya
mukhe jwalamalini hrim hrim hrim hram hram hrom hrah sarva
grahanam hridaye daha daha pach pach chhindi chhindi bhindi
bhindi daha daha ha ha sphut sphut the the.*

*Kshmalum ksham kshim kshaum kshaum kshah stambhapah
mumlum brhram bhrim bhrim bhrum bhraim bhraum bhraih
badaya badaya. Mumlum bhram bhrim bhrum braim bhrauam
bhrah netram sphotaya sphotaya darshaya darshaya. Yumlum
yam yim yaim yaum yah preshaya preshaya gmulum ghram
ghram ghram ghrim ghrum grhaim ghraum ghrah jatharam
bhedaya bhedaya gmlum gram grim graum graim graum grah
mukhai bandhaya bandhaya. Rkyum kham khim khum khaim
khaum khah grivam bhanjaya bhanjaya. Chhplum chham chhim
chhum chhaim chhaum chhah antran bhedaya bhedaya. Drplum
dram drim drum draim drauam draha mahavidyu tapamana*

*strahanshtraihan vmpum vram vrim vrum vraim vraum vrah
samudre manjay manjay drampum dram drim drum draim draum
draha sarva dakinim sundarim mardaya mardaya sarva yogini
svajjaiya svajjaiya. Sarva shatrum grasaya grasaya kha kha
kha kha kha kha kha khadaya khadaya sarva daityan vidhvansaya
vidhvansaya sarva mrityum nashaya nashaya sarvopadravan
stambhaya stambhaya jah jah jah jah jah jah jah javaran daha
daha pach pach ghumu ghumu ghuru ghuru kharu khau khang
ravana suvidyayan ghataya ghataya akhila rujan doshodayan
krita karyanabhicharotthana (amukasya) deha sthitan adhuna
ruj karankan chandrahas shastrena chhedaya chhedaya bhedaya
bhedaya uru uru chharu chharu sphut sphut ghe am kraum
kshim ksham kshaim kshaum kshah jwala malini (amukasya)
sankhyam kurukuru nirujam kurukuru abhilashit kamana dehi
dehi jwala malini vigyapataye swaha.*

VOCABULARY

Aum	Aum
Astra	Weapon
Ashtra Asan	A seat made of weapon
Bahri	External
Bhairon	Deity of Hindus
Bhuddhism	Name of the religion
Baheda	A fruit used medicinally
Brahma	Deity of Hindus
Bhimsottari	A big rope
Chhotti Elachi	Cardamom
Chinna	Disease
Dhoti-Kurta	A piece of cloth worn around the lower body-shirt
Durga	Deity of Hindus
Guru	Teacher
Hridya	Heart
Hasta	Hand
Jainism	Religious name
Jata Dhari	A person with long hairs
Jyotish	Astrology

Japa	Recitation
Karma	Fate
Kashmira	Pertaining to truth & purity
Kavash	Armour
Kauravas	Descendants of Kuru
Kshtriya	A community of the Hindus
Kaam	Sex
Kubera	Lord of wealth
Kritika	The third Lunar month
Kaaryothsrag	To stand in water for meditation
Karan Pisachini	Female devil who convey message in ear
Krodh Shanti Mantra	Mantra to control temper
Kanishta	Smallest finger known as mercury finger
Lakshmi	Goddess of wealth
Long	Clove
Lord Vishnu	Deity of Hindus
Lord Varuna	Deity of Hindus
Lord Shiva	Deity of Hindus
Maharishis	Great Saints
Mantra Maha Nivarana	Epic
Mantramohodhdhi	Epic
Mantra Parijata	Epic
Mantra Sarvasava	Epic

Maaran	To destroy
Mantra Shakti	Power of Mantra
Mantroddhara	Extraction from holy concept
Maya	Illusion
Maathrka	A religious way
Maun Varta	To remain mum for long time
Mantraism	Recitation of couplet
Mantra	A sacred verse
Mantra Datta	Guru who gives Mantra
Mrigchala	Skin of Deer
Mahabharata	A great war of Bharat
Netra	Eye
Navrattan	Nine gems including Ruby, Pearl, Emrald, Coral, Blue Sapphire, Topaz, Gomed and Cats eye
OM Namo Shivaye	A sacred couplet enchanted in the praise of Hindu God Shiva
Om Namo Narayanaya	A sacred couplet enchanted in the praise of Hindu God Narayanaya
Pandavas	Descendants of high class learned community (Pandu)
Purascharana	Repetition
Paran Mukha	Disease
Pala	Moment

Parvani	The highest pitch of sound in enchanting Mantra
Rishis	Saints
Ruddha	Disease
Rashi	Zodiac sign
Rohini	Name of planetary hour
Rudraksh	Dry flower of holy tree which is used for making of rosary
Rakta Hina	(Without blood)
Roti	(Bread)
Rama	The name of Hindu God
Shastra	A Scripture
Sadhna	Practice of occultism
Shree Orgin	To start
Sadhaka	Practitioner
Sarv Siddhi	To attain power
Sattvika	Pertaining to truth & purity
Shan Asha	Ray of hope
Sharvana	Period comes between the month of June-July
Sarwasta	Every body
Suraya	Sun
Sarswati Ma	Deity of Education
Saiva	At once service
Sakta	An able performer

SA-RE-GA-MA-PA-DHA-NI	Sapta Swaras, Seven codes of music
Supta	Disease
Shanti	Peace
Tarajani	First finger adjoining the thumb known as Jupiter finger
Tantric	A practitioner
Trishul	Weapon of Lord Shiva
Uttaraphalguni	The eleventh & twelfth lunar asterism
Uttaraadha	Last hour of day or script
Uchhattan	Recitation
Vama Marga	The left hand way
Vashikarana Mantra	Mantra for attraction
Vedas	Vedas
Vidya	Education
Vidmaska (page 27)	Ability to over come the situation
Vaishnava	Vegetarian
Visirna	Disease
Vipala	Fraction of moment
Yash Prapti	To attain name and fame

PRACTICAL ASTROLOGY

By

Alan Leo

People, everywhere and always, have believed that the stars govern their destinies. History records that sooth-sayers in royal courts used to interpret the message of the stars for kings. Mystified, the people linked astrology to religion. But it was much more—a religo-scientific subject. PRACTICAL ASTROLOGY written after extensive investigation tries to tell the reader that in "the methaphysical alone can be found the abstract cause for the concrete event" in anybody's life and, therefore, it alone can "help him understand himself".

The book in a lucid style unravels the celestial laws and the ways they govern the solar system i.e. every thing and every event every time every where.

ISBN : 81-242-0221-4   Price : Rs. 125/-

HEALING THROUGH YANTRA

By

P. Khurrana

The author P.Khurrana is a great spiritual healer whose work has been appreciated in India and abroad. And he has devoted his life to the study of Jantra-Tantra- Mantra since the age of 18. In the present book the author has written about the power and strength of Yantra. P. Khurrana's study about Yantra is completely based on his deep research work.

The book is distinguished and has been written in a very simple and understanding manner. Author describes that the life is a complex combination of incidents and accidents but one can definitely find relief through miracles of Yantras.

ISBN :81-242-0172-2   Price : Rs. 125/-

UNDERSTANDING ASTROLOGY

By

W. Frankland

ASTROLOGY is the Science that investigates the action and reaction existing between the Heavenly bodies and the rest of manifested Nature, including Man Astrology reveals the Laws under which this takes place.

It reaches One Law, One Life, in varying forms that are the manifestation of the One Universal Spirit.

It enables Man to know himself, to grapple with his nature. It enables him to take the most of his abilities.

It is further affords him a clue to the direction he is likely to take in various affairs of life. It indexes the conditions to be encountered.

If therefore he understands it and to the extent he understands it, the Horoscope proves a chart and compass in life.

ISBN : 81-242-0104-8   Price : Rs. 40/-

MOON-SUN
&
ASTROLOGY

By

P. Khurrana

The moon & the Sun are the great mysterious planets, proclaiming the incalculable wonders to Divine Design. The Moon and the Sun happen to be the only planets which are luminous in character. All the rest are opaque. Hence Astrology without the study of these two great planets remains incomplete.

How the Moon-Sun influence goes to have an effect on the physical, enviornmental aspects of a human being's life has been dealt with, in this book.

ISBN : 81-242-0134-X   Price : Rs. 95.00